AFRICA IN TRANSITION

AFRICA
IN TRANSITION

SOME BBC TALKS ON CHANGING

CONDITIONS IN THE UNION

AND THE RHODESIAS

★

Edited by Prudence Smith

MAX REINHARDT · LONDON

First published by
Max Reinhardt Limited
10 *Earlham Street*
*London, W.C.*2

©

PRUDENCE SMITH
1958

Made and printed in England by
STAPLES PRINTERS LIMITED
at their Rochester, Kent, establishment

CONTENTS

(Except where otherwise stated the talks refer in the main to conditions and research in the Union of South Africa.)

v

14013

EDITOR'S PREFACE

From August to December 1955 I travelled, on behalf of the BBC Talks Department, in most of the territories from the Belgian Congo through East and Central Africa to the Cape. I visited in particular the many centres where the social, cultural and economic problems of Africa are studied, and also saw many practical projects for development, rehabilitation, housing, health and welfare in both rural and urban areas. I was, of course, in search of broadcasts, programmes which would comprise not a survey of the problems or the territories, but which would offer a series of insights into them based upon the research and long experience of people who live and work in these countries.' So rich was the field and such the keenness and kindness on all sides that in the following year the Third Programme was able to broadcast a series of 51 programmes, spread over three months, all of them truly 'new out of Africa'.

This book presents, in the main, a selection of those talks which dealt specifically with the impact of the presence and institutions of Europeans upon the African peoples of the Union of South Africa and the Rhodesias. It is therefore about 'race relations' in the widest meaning of that much-used term; indeed it is hoped that these talks may show how wide, and how various, its implications are.

Broadcast talks of this kind are neither learned articles warmed up nor popular articles cooled down. The transitory nature of the medium need not conflict with the serious intent of speakers and listeners. The very danger of this conflict often produces its resolution in a rare and valuable kind of communication: that is, a talk in which a specialist speaks about his work in some detail but offers his interpretation or conclusion mindful that listeners will want to relate what he says to the wider, more general picture which they gain from other sources, not least the daily Press. In presenting these talks therefore, in permanent printed form, no effort has been made to change their nature by devices which would incline them either to the learned or the popular side. The temptation to include footnote references was strong, but resisted, and in partial recompense a brief reading list has been included of works immediately relevant. The contributors have brought some passages up to date in the light of developments of research since the time of broadcasting. Some of the talks have been slightly shortened and, to avoid repetitiousness in the book, shorn of passages on aspects more fully developed by other contributors.

Only one kind of omission from the original series must be mentioned. There was a section of prepared debates in which leading Afrikaners gave their views about different aspects of the *apartheid* policy, which were in turn criticized by other speakers. Of this section, though highly relevant to the theme of the book, only two talks are included, simply because South African legislation since 1955, proposed and actual, has rendered them out of date. The two which remain are by social scientists, Professor Olivier and Dr Hellman, and are concerned with the general theory rather than the detailed implementation of the *apartheid* policy. It should perhaps be stressed that neither of these contributors is the spokesman of a political party.

The book ends with three talks of a different kind, personal reflections of an African, a Coloured and an Asian speaker because they are men who in many ways live at the heart of the cultural conflict which the book is about.

The broadcasting enterprise and therefore this book would not have been possible without the help and advice of many people and organizations, especially in Africa. They are too numerous to name, but I should like to repeat none the less sincerely the thanks I have already expressed to them on behalf of the BBC; and to stress that the selection of broadcasts here published owed a particular debt to the technical co-operation of the South African Broadcasting Corporation and the Federal Broadcasting Corporation of Rhodesia and Nyasaland.

Finally, since this is not a BBC publication, I welcome the opportunity of saying that from first to last the project has owed immeasurably to the lively interest and support of Mary Somerville, formerly BBC Controller of Talks, and of John Morris, Controller of the Third Programme.

PRUDENCE SMITH

London, July 1957

I

INTRODUCTION:

GOVERNMENT IN A CHANGING AFRICA

by The Rt. Hon. the Lord Hailey

G.C.S.I., G.C.M.G., G.C.I.E.

f I were asked what part of Africa would today provide the most interesting study, I should find it hard to decide. Would it be North Africa, where Egypt is thrusting itself into the medley of international politics, and Algeria is illustrating in the crudest form the stresses which may have to be faced by the government of a country of mixed peoples? Or would it be West Africa, hot in the pursuit of self-determination? Or would it be hat line of countries running up from the Union into East Africa, where the pressure of economic development seems to have led so many to overlook the need for dispassionate thought on the problem of race relations?

The series of talks which I am introducing has taken the last group of countries for its field. If this has narrowed its scope, it has nevertheless secured one great advantage. It has made it possible to illustrate different aspects in the life of these countries by talks from men and women nearly all of whom are actually resident in them. The topics on which they contribute are for them not merely matters of academic study, but are part of their own lives.

If I myself now emphasize a more general aspect of the situation in these countries, it is because I feel that it is one which lies in the background of all of the problems which those who follow me will proceed to discuss. I put it simply as follows. Everywhere the African, in the sense of the indigenous people of Africa, is today asserting for himself a much more dramatic part in the complex of Africa's problems. When I look back on the Africa which I began to study a few years before the outbreak of the war, I realize that the problems which then presented themselves were the problems as Europeans saw them. The solutions which we debated were no doubt those which we believed at the time to be best for Africans. But Europeans were to take the lead in working them out, and it was to be Europeans who would, within reason, have the last voice in their settlement.

That picture is no longer true today. Every year that passes now sees the African himself fill a more important rôle in the developing drama of Africa. I do not wish to exaggerate the position. I do not suggest that the rising spirit of Africanism, if I may use that expression, is the outcome of a general movement or is inspired by a common purpose. On the contrary, it has a diversity as manifest as that of the different regions of Africa. It is inevitable, moreover, that it should reflect something of the differences in the political philosophies of the European governments which continue to control so large a part of the continent.

I will take my illustration of this position as far as possible from within the area which is the subject of the present series of talks. In the Union of South Africa the standards of life of the African community are relatively higher than those of its neighbours, but they depend pre-eminently on the part which Africans play in the economic life of the European community. It is difficult to see how the African can hope in any foreseeable future either to gain control of this source of material development or to replace it. He needs the European just as much as the

European needs him. But he knows that even the most extreme apostle of the gospel of segregation cannot today envisage a future in which Africans can be hived off into a completely separate native state or states. He knows also that in the industrial life of the Union he is every year increasing his own quota in the ranks of semi-skilled if not of skilled labour. What then must be his outlook on his future? Clearly it must lie in so improving his status within the economic life of the European community, that he will be able to assert an unanswerable claim to take a larger share in the political life of the Union.

There must be many in this country who wonder why the late years have seen what might almost be described as a militant effort on the part of the Union Government to ensure the practical application of the doctrine of segregation. I feel that the explanation lies in the growing realization by the European community of the situation created by the post-war advance of Africans in the field of industry. I would add that it is an advantage that the long and painstaking investigations of the Tomlinson Commission have now given us an objective view of some of the implications involved in further efforts to give substance to the principle of segregation, more particularly in respect of the measures needed in order to raise the standard of living in the Native Reserves.

Africans in Southern Rhodesia are not in the same degree dependent on improving their share in the economic life of the European community. Their outlook is at the moment directed to securing an increase in the proportion of political representation now accorded to them. This, as they see it, can eventually be used by them to obtain a larger share in the social and other services provided by the State.

If I were to trespass outside the field with which this series of talks will deal, I could readily find instances, as for example, in British West Africa, where the African community is far more confident of itself, and has gone much further in asserting its claims. But my point is already clear. The rising spirit of Africanism may vary from country to country in strength and direction. But taking it as a whole, it adds up to something very different from anything that a previous generation knew in its dealing with African affairs.

What is the reaction of the different governments to this development? Over some of these governments, as for instance those in East Africa, Great Britain still has a measure of control. Over others, as Southern Rhodesia, the extent of its control is now almost negligible. Over the Union our control has ceased to exist in any form, though there are some well meaning people in Britain who do not seem as yet to have appreciated this fact. But it is in dealing with the current policy of the Union that our public needs to be in special measure realistic. It is necessary for it to realize that *apartheid* is not by any means a doctrine that is held only by a reactionary section of the white population. The dynamic behind it lies in the honest conviction that unless one is prepared to see a reduction in the standards of life established by the European community, it is essential to maintain inviolate the supremacy of Europeans in the political and social life of the country. There may be differences in the views held by different parties regarding the working of what has now come to be known as the operative application of segregation, but there seems to be little question that the majority of Europeans in the Union will stand together in asserting the principle of European supremacy. But whether the substance of the doctrine of segregation can in fact be maintained in the future seems to me to depend on the answer to one crucial question. The industries of the Union now make a larger contribution to the national income than its mines or its agriculture. Can an industrialized Union *afford* to maintain the political and social segregation of the labour which has now become vital to its existence? I think that we in this country should be content to await the effect of the impact of economic forces on the political outlook of the dominant European community.

Then take Southern Rhodesia. Here also I think we need to be realistic, though the oustanding problem differs very materially from that of the Union. In Southern Rhodesia the constitution has from the first provided that the African shall, if he has the necessary franchise qualifications, have access to the vote. But this has up to date resulted in the exercise by Africans of a minimum of voting power. The declared policy of the Federation of Rhodesia and Nyasaland is that of "partnership", but there have been incidents which give rise to some doubt whether Europeans are in fact as firmly united in the determination to give effect to the doctrine of partnership as the Europeans of the Union are united in an opposite direction. It would be unfortunate if there should now occur any widening of the differences which have begun to appear in the front presented by the European community in support of this principle. The test will be seen in the decisions arrived at on the deliberations in the Federation regarding the procedure to be adopted for the extension of the franchise to Africans. There has, I would add, been one measure of great importance to Africans recently placed on the statute book in Southern Rhodesia. This has initiated a scheme of rural improvement which will not merely place African peasants throughout the country in possession of individual holdings, in place of their former communal tenure, but will expend considerable sums in assisting them to improve their production. That may mean a far-reaching change in African village life, and it must inevitably increase the number of Africans who will qualify for the vote.

It is not today possible to dwell on problems such as these without at the same time taking account of developments which are occurring in other parts of Africa, and at the present moment much of the attention of the British people is naturally attracted by the Independence of Ghana to the drama which is being enacted in our West African dependencies. There Great Britain is engaged in extending to them a self-governing status which follows the pattern of the Parliamentary form of government with which we ourselves are familiar. There are those who have been inclined to complain that we have failed to realize that there may be other forms of government which are perhaps better suited to the conditions of Africa. That is true; but it may also be said that we are giving to these dependencies something in which our national experience has led us to place our own faith. For that reason, if for no other, we ought perhaps to be able to give Africans more help in the introduction and working of this system than we could if we adopted any alternative form of government.

Nevertheless, it is often suggested that we ought to introduce a different form of administration in our colonial dependencies, and should employ civil servants who have a different type of approach towards the needs of Africans. But it seems too late in the day to suggest alterations of system now. Constitutional change is no longer a steady march; it moves at a gallop. Moreover, I do not myself know from what source we could obtain those paragons who could do so much more to help Africans than the existing services have been able to achieve.

Here also however I wish to be realistic. I see now a series of colonies, that are on the brink of attaining self-rule, but with little personnel of their own who have been definitely equipped to discharge the responsibilities of administration. That is a function which in an undeveloped country is perhaps of greater concern to the people at large than the possession of leading men who are competent in the field of politics. I reflect that when we resigned control in India there was no such

iatus. For over a generation before the transfer of power we
had been giving to Indians the same range of duties and
responsibilities as to men who had been recruited in this
country. I can look with pride on the work now being done in
India by Indians whom I knew as my colleagues in the administrative services. I fear that we shall leave behind us no
comparable legacy in Africa.

PART ONE

★

2

MALNUTRITION IN AFRICAN CONDITIONS

by *Theodore Gillman*

I imagine that many of us, if asked to give a general impression of the people of Africa, would envisage badly housed, disease-ridden and starving millions. For the black people this is largely true, except in one important respect – frank starvation is not a basic health problem in Africa. Starvation kills, but chronic malnutrition insidiously erodes the health of the people and this is, perhaps, the most significant single factor directly and indirectly retarding African progress.

Malnutrition among a population is like an iceberg in the sense that only a small part of the whole is readily visible. So it is to be expected that when, as occurs in Africa, a small proportion of the people regularly presents itself at hospitals in frank and acute nutritional failure, the majority, even of the seemingly healthy, will be found to suffer from chronic malnutrition. Post mortem examinations on apparently healthy Africans killed in accidents almost invariably reveal widespread bodily damage, due directly or indirectly to the consumption of a grossly unsatisfactory diet.

We lack adequate statistics, but there are a few which will serve to sketch a rough pattern of life and death for Africans. These figures are taken from South Africa, but what I have to say applies in large measure to the continent as a whole. The average life expectancy of the African in the Union is estimated as 36 years. That among the European population is the same as for Britain, about 70. On the Witwatersrand, that is to say a large urbanized area, where the death rate among Europeans was 7.6 per thousand, that for Africans was 20.9. Sixty-seven per cent of these African deaths were attributable to diseases associated with malnutrition. In a large rural area, the Ciskei Native Reserve, a recent survey shows that of a thousand African infants born alive, 242 died before the age of 1 year, 327 before 2 years, and 508 before they were 18.

The low life expectancy and high morbidity among the African people is obviously attributable to many socio-economic causes and cannot presently be regarded as a peculiar racial feature. Chronic malnutrition from infancy, and even from conception, is, as I have said, certainly among the most important direct and indirect factors sapping the vitality of the pigmented peoples of Africa. Several surveys among African school children have revealed that from 60% to 70% are recognizably malnourished; 50% need nursing and medical attention, while almost 10% of children attending school may require hospitalization for diseases directly or indirectly attributable to malnutrition. With this background in infancy and childhood, it is not really suprising that in Northern Rhodesia the average weight of the adult male has been reported to be ten pounds lower than the European standard for the same height. Of Africans from Native territories applying for work on the gold mines between 1940 and 1943, 25% were rejected as physically unfit.

Now the scientist must grapple with this gigantic and appalling problem before the doctor or administrator or employer can take any steps. We must first be clear about what we mean by malnutrition, and at the outset one must, in all honesty, say that despite the rapid advances in our knowledge of the chemistry of foods during the past two or three decades, we are still not able to state what is the ideal diet for human beings at

ifferent ages and under different physical and climatic condi-
ons. We lack precise knowledge of the ways in which the
ods we eat affect us, for good or ill.

You have all heard that you need a certain number of
alories of energy per day from food and a minimum amount
f one or other protein, fat, vitamin or mineral. You, in the
Jnited Kingdom, could hardly avoid learning something of
utrition during the 'hungry forties'. But whatever you were
old, or asked to do, was the best nutritionists had to offer at
hat time. This was indubitably helpful, but all concerned in
efining policy will, I am sure, readily agree that it was their
est guess in your interests, rather than precise irrefutable
act.

We all know, too, that by manipulating their diet, pigs,
ows and fowls can be made to produce bacon more rapidly,
ield more milk, or lay more eggs. It is possible, then, to
nodify the weight, height, adiposity and other characteristics
f many species by dietary means. Similarly, under carefully-
ontrolled experimental conditions, it is also possible signifi-
antly to increase or decrease the incidence and age of onset of
nany diseases, such as cancers, heart, vascular and kidney
isease, and in genetically pure strains, even to increase or
horten the average life span of experimental animals. Since
he disease incidence and life span of a specific population of
nimals can be profoundly modified by their diet, it is justifi-
ble to suggest that the same may hold true for man. This is
upported by recent studies which have revealed a close relation
etween the caloric intake, and especially the fat content of the
iet, of seemingly well-nourished human beings, and the
requency and early onset of coronary and other arterial
iseases. Recent statistics show, for example, that in the U.S.A.,
y average standards, 35 millions (more than one-fifth) of the
opulation of 165 million are overweight, 15 million by 20%

and 20 million by 10%. Such obesity is strongly suspected t predispose to diabetes, arterio-sclerosis and kidney diseases.

The majority of African people consume diets which ar inadequate both in quantity *and* in quality. So-called specifi vitamin deficiency diseases are extremely common.

As for quality – some confusion exists in the minds of th public and even of many nutritionists. It is of the greate importance to realize that specific deficiency diseases ca experimentally be produced in healthy animals only if a ver special combination of foodstuffs is fed. Under these circum stances, the absence of a single factor (A) may result in the pro duction of a particular disease or lesion, but if the constituen of this very special diet (other than A) are altered, then th specific diseases attributed to the original absence of A ma not, and frequently do not emerge.

In other words it is not only what is missing from the die that is significant, but also what is present, and especially th combinations of nutrients. To take a simple example fror some of our own experiments: if rats are fed, *ad lib.*, only o mealie meal porridge, they remained dwarfed, live for 12 t 18 weeks, but fail to develop any obvious diseases; they ar simply starved and stunted. However, if 10% of brewer yeast, an excellent source of vitamin B complex and of veget able protein, is added to the mealie meal, the rats may grov quite rapidly, but almost 100% develop severe rickets wit gross bony distortions in 8 to 10 weeks. Other diseases can b induced in rats eating a predominantly mealie meal diet, b adding allegedly good nutrients such as milk powder, soy bean meal and vegetables. This is especially so *if only one* c these allegedly good foods is added to the grossly unsatisfactor mealie meal diet.

There are many other experiments recorded in the scientifi literature proving that to supplement an inadequate diet, solel on the basis of its chemically determined constitution and without meticulous attention to the biological actions of its component foods, may increase the severity of the primary inadequacies of that diet. Moreover, it is now well established that harmful or even frankly toxic effects can result from the addition of an excess of one allegedly good nutrient to an inadequate diet, especially when consumed by an already malnourished individual.

The relevance of this to the human problem will be clear. Human beings eat natural foods, and each of these is a complex package of chemical substances having its own peculiar metabolic effects which increase the individual's requirements for other nutrients. This holds particularly for maize and rice which are common staple foods of backward people. The upshot is that the addition of seemingly good foods to inadequate diets, comprised primarily of single staple foods, can precipitate disease. At least until we are fully acquainted with the metabolic effects and special needs evoked by the qualitatively inadequate diets which are the rule in Africa, we cannot easily recommend single or even multiple artificial supplements, purely on the basis of chemical analysis of these diets.

Starving people do not develop degeneratory nutritional diseases, like pellagra or beri-beri. They are not consuming enough to be stimulated metabolically to the point where they break down with deficiency diseases. The inmates of Belsen and other concentration camps were virtually free of scurvy, pellagra and other nutritional syndromes. For the most part they simply burnt their own body tissues to provide the minimal energy needed to maintain essential life processes, thus gradually wasting away to death.

The reasonable conclusion to be drawn from both animal experiments and human evidence is, that to develop degeneratory nutritional diseases, it is necessary to eat enough food of inadequate quality. This is what occurs in most backward countries, like Africa.

To come to the awkward question of defining malnutrition, I would like, on the basis of these considerations, to suggest as a working definition that any individual is malnourished if he consumes a diet which actively promotes degeneratory diseases. Thus overweight Americans who develop fatal cardiac and other diseases prematurely, are malnourished, albeit in a way quite different from the underweight, stunted African, who develops pellagra or chronic liver diseases, who is unduly susceptible to infection and who dies before the age of forty.

It is not scientifically justifiable to regard the African pellagrin as suffering from an *acute* deficiency disease curable in a short while with single or even with multiple vitamin supplements. His diet is deficient quantitatively, that is, in calories, as well as vitamins. His diet is also grossly unbalanced, in that his staple foods, such as maize, cassava or plantains, are defective in many respects and force his body to metabolize such foods in particular ways, thereby promoting the need for additional foodstuffs – about which we still know too little to be practically helpful.

A true perspective on the effects of chronic malnutrition can only be attained if attention is diverted from the rather startling acute episodes of nutritional collapse among adult Africans. The effects of chronic malnutrition are less obvious, but more subtle, more fundamental and far more devastating. The mothers are malnourished from their infancy and, with the physiological strains imposed by childbearing, become progressively more so, ageing rapidly with each succeeding pregnancy. Consequently, even the foetus may be malnourished. It is not to be wondered at that African babies are born underweight, are hypersusceptible to the many infective diseases in their slum environments, and succumb to these so

sily and so often. From his mother's breast the baby is weaned
a to a pabulum which inevitably brings degeneration, acutely
slowly. Professor Trowell, of Kampala, once wrote: 'No one
Britain would regard it as satisfactory if a child was weaned
n a diet of bread and water, but the position of such a child
ould be fortunate in comparison with many young children
the tropics.'

With such an unsatisfactory nutritional background, it is very
urprising that if he does survive beyond the age of 3 years, the
frican child between the ages of 4 and 14, whilst stunted and
eak, nevertheless seems immune to acute nutritional break-
owns. Yet, the later history of such children reveals how
early they have paid to maintain such immunity.

At 20 to 25, to those inexperienced in dealing with Africans,
ey look 20 to 30 years older. They present themselves at
ospitals by the tens of thousands, with chronic and, at present,
ucurable liver diseases, with premature heart failure and
equently apathetic or even demented. Strangely enough
ancers, apart from those affecting the female breast and
enital tract, are relatively rare among the Africans. This may
ell be due to the fact that the African simply fails to live to
ie more advanced age when cancers are most common in
uropeans. However, when the African male does develop
ancer, it afflicts him between the ages of 15 and 35, and then
iost frequently it is primary cancer of his liver – a condition
xtremely rare among Europeans.

There are many too, who claim that the African's mind is
iferior to that of the European. Apart from the inadequate
ome environment and poor school facilities, the mental
uggishness which the African often does seem to manifest
iay be expected purely on nutritional grounds. I mentioned
iat chronic, progressive liver diseases are among the most
equent repercussions of life-long malnutrition on the African.

It is known that in the presence of *non*-nutritional chronic liv
disease, the brain is often simultaneously damaged. Thus, in tl
African, low grade chronic cerebral damage may well be du
indirectly to chronic malnutritional liver diseases. In view o
this, and of many other adverse environmental factors, it
quite unjustifiable to regard the African as *inheriting* an inferio
mental capacity.

What he does inherit is a way of living which virtuall
commits him to a life pattern which invites physical an
mental catastrophe. We are forced to recognize that whe
Africans present themselves at hospitals in frank nutrition
failure, widely regarded as acute deficiency diseases, it is foo
hardy to think of curing them by short-term treatment wi
large doses of vitamin concentrates. The acute symptoms an
signs may, indeed, be resolved by such treatment – combine
with the best of all medical treatments, namely, rest in bed
but the chronic damage persists and progresses.

The nutritionally determined life pattern of the Africa
condemns him to premature death in infancy, or, should l
survive, to premature senility and susceptibility, two to thr
decades earlier, to many diseases which afflict better nourishe
populations between the ages of 50 and 70.

How then are we to deal with this grave and urgent problen
How to rehabilitate those surviving despite the chronic an
progressive damage they harbour? I cannot avoid concludin;
however sadly, that for the diffusely injured adult, little can l
done apart from providing him with nutritional crutches.

You may say that it would be both humanely and econom
cally desirable, even as an interim measure, to tinker with tl
grossly inadequate diets of the majority of Africans, by addin
one or more nutrients in the hope at least of ameliorating
critical situation. But we still do not know *how* to improve suc
diets by supplements, especially if, as in Africa, a single natur

od is used as a staple comprising more than 75% to 80% of the tal caloric intake. In our attempts to find such simple supplements, which could with *safety* be added to diets comprised rimarily of maize, or of other staples, we have conducted erally hundreds of experiments in animals.

And until we do find the answers, we are confounded by the mple evidence substantiating the view – first put forward ten ears ago from this country – that, *in the wrong dietary setting,* good food may indeed *promote* disease. It seems to me necessary, in our present ignorance, to warn against such steps. here is scarcely any other known stimulus capable of proking such chronic illhealth as a monotonous and inferior iet. There is scarcely any other way whereby it is possible, ittingly or unwittingly, to inflict such widespread bodily arm on so many people as by tampering, incorrectly, with a ition's diet.

Yet the situation is not entirely hopeless. Much *can* be done Africa even today, if we attend vigorously to the pregnant others, new-born infants and to the children. But we must cognize that nothing short of a major change in the feeding f the pregnant women and their offspring will yield reliable d satisfactory results.

The present tasks of nutritional science are to determine the recise relations between dietary habits, longevity and the egenerative processes of ageing; the effects on health of the anifold chemical and physical treatments involved in rocessing common foods; the influences of dietary habits on ficiency, productivity and resistance to infections and the nstitution of the diets most favourable to human growth and evelopment, at all ages from prenatal life through to old age.

Although we still do not know what is an ideal diet for man, e do know of diets better than those presently consumed by e majority of Africans. In essence, we must aim at eliminating

the monotony of the diet, comprised, as it is, predominantly
a single food. The diet should be constituted of a variety
natural foods – eggs, bread, butter, milk, meat, fish, vegetabl
and the like, in quantities sufficient to make maize or any oth
staple comprise a much smaller part of the total food consume

But if you know the poverty and economic backwardness
Africa, it is at once apparent that the elimination of chron
malnutrition is no longer the task of the nutritional researc
worker, except in so far as he may be able to advise th
politicians and the technologists. It is upon their shoulde
that the responsibility now rests.

3

HEALTH AND CULTURAL CHANGE

by Sidney L. Kark

Greater and greater areas of Africa are being drawn into the industrial revolution. That is the economists' way of saying that in such areas every African man, woman and child is obliged to make profound changes in his daily living, changes more sudden and probably more difficult in every way than were thrust upon people in Britain during the late eighteenth and the nineteenth centuries. It is not surprising that some major health problems have emerged from the process; in fact they have been created or greatly magnified by it.

I am not going to deal with diseases which are an obvious direct consequence of the squalor and poverty of an urban slum environment, but with a rural African community in which my wife and I worked for several years and established a health centre, which happened to be the first in South Africa.

This Zulu-speaking community of people lives in Pholela, a magisterial area of south-western Natal, in the foothills of the Drakensberg. It is a district of deep valleys with fast flowing rivers and rugged mountains stripped of their vegetation. In the valleys and lower slopes of these foothills the people keep their poorly cultivated fields, dominated by the mealie (or maize), their staple food. Cattle and goats graze on the scanty vegetation of the ridges and upper slopes of the mountains.

The countryside is at once beautiful, imposing and tragic; beautiful in its grandeur and harshness, tragic in the devastation brought by soil erosion. Where once there may have bee indigenous forest and lush veld, sheet erosion has expose subsoil and rock, and gullies have torn their way through th grazing lands, between the lines of homesteads, and deep int the fields below. The climate is bracing, at an altitude of fron four to six thousand feet above sea-level; the winter days ar sunny, though cold winds come from the snow-cappe Drakensberg; summer rains are heavy and the mists smoot the harshness of the steep mountain slopes. All these thing present a physical challenge which might have been turned t good account by a people with deep-rooted peasant tradition

But the Pholela people's response has been largely deter mined by the industrial development of South Africa. Instea of meeting the challenge at home, men look to the towns fc employment, and their main occupation is wage earning a migratory labourers in the growing industrial centres. Tradi tional forms of labour undertaken by men in their triba society remain important features of Pholela, but cannot b regarded as anything else than supplementary to their mai function of earning money in the towns.

So that miles away from Pholela, and yet part of it, lie th towns where there are many features similar to the towns c Europe during the industrial revolution. Large towns appeare suddenly with hastily constructed, poorly-planned dwelling ill-lit, badly ventilated and generally unaesthetic. For th people thus 'urbanized', the whole process has meant th growth of a new way of life under circumstances hardly con ducive to health; in South Africa acute enteritis of infants an enteric fever are the diseases analogous to the destructiv cholera and enteritis outbreaks in countries like Britain in th nineteenth century. Tuberculosis and pneumonia reach epi demic proportions, and smallpox and typhus outbreaks becam common under such conditions.

The unhygienic personal life was not only directly related to the inadequate housing and sanitation, but was an important reflection of adjustment to the new system of social relationships involved in urbanization. Not only did new social institutions appear, such as the mine and the factory, involving difficult problems of adjustment for the individual workers but old institutions were modified in their function.

This is well illustrated in the change which took place in the functions of the family, which in its rural and village setting was an economic production unit, whereas in the new urban area this function was increasingly removed from the home to the factory. The changed function of the family inevitably led to changes in the relationship between husbands and wives, and a change in the position of children within the home. Maladjustment in personal relations became manifest and gross forms of delinquency were very common.

Such conditions are mainly of historical interest in Britain; in South Africa they are part of present-day life.

But the outstanding feature of the South African situation, in which it differs from that of most other countries undergoing industrialization, is the persistence of the temporary migrant labour system. And so in considering the implications of this persistent feature, it will be realized that Pholela society is not rural in the full meaning of the term. So many of the men are normally occupied in urban employment that this aspect of their lives must be taken into account. While in the urban area they are not only involved in relationships with their employers, but with large numbers of other people in the streets, buses, trains, shops and market places, with Europeans, Coloured people, Asiatics, and various tribal groups of Africans, with foreign languages and habits. These manifold social relationships, while not a part of Pholela life as geographically defined, must be regarded as part of its life as socially defined; and without

B

this concept of Pholela as a complex of rural and urban processes, one cannot understand the factors influencing its well-being and the incidence of ill-health in the community.

The main pillars of Pholela's economy are local food production, in which women play the major rôle, and wage-earning in the towns by the men. Together, these two economic activities fail to meet the elementary needs of the community. Food consumption studies and clinical investigations show inadequacy of diet associated with poor growth and nutritional failure syndromes. But the immediate nutritional implications of this unsound economy, important as they are, are by no means the only unfortunate effects. The disturbed human relationships, particularly noted in family relations, result in profound emotional disturbances which are so often manifested in crises of individual maladjustment as well as in nutritional failure.

In comparatively stable societies, where social change takes place gradually, the medical profession is of course very alive to the psychosomatic nature of many illnesses, and in such societies it is often difficult enough to determine the causes of a patient's maladjustment. In African communities such as Pholela the task is immeasurably greater especially as the European doctor has rarely had training in the social sciences and often has little opportunity to acquire an adequate knowledge of his patients' language.

As for the African, having been reared for one set of circumstances with values of a particular period, he finds himself in a different situation which itself demands flexibility and initiative because of its changing nature. His tribal *mores* no longer have meaning or give him guidance in his actual experience. Not only is a state of conflict engendered in respect of his moral values, but relationships with others become more difficult to define. His tribal relationships are mainly within the framework of a primary social unit, where his contacts are face-to-face, intimate, and have continuity. When he moves to the town a variety of less intimate relationships play an increasing part and his previous experience may actually hamper his adjustment. He becomes uncertain of his own rôle and of nearly all his relationships, including those with his own family when at length he returns to them.

Professor Marwick discusses, elsewhere in this book, the continued and increasing part of witchcraft beliefs, to which the African resorts in an attempt to ease the tensions of his changing world. My medical experience certainly supports these findings. So often when a man becomes ill he begins to think of who would wish him harm, or of what it is that he has not done that he ought to have done, for which his ancestors are now punishing him.

But he has not only his tribal community to think of. He has in his urban employment entered into many situations of stress and new relationships, any one of which may well constitute a challenge beyond his capacity, and whether he is in Pholela, or, say, Johannesburg at the time, he seeks the help of his traditional practitioner. The skills of this practitioner himself, developed within a society in which primary group relations were the 'all' of man's social living, are extended to the new complexity of relationships within which both the practitioner and his patient may now live. The extension of witchcraft beliefs is in reality a natural result of the extension of the area of stress and unresolved conflict, far beyond that which was known in tribal society.

Now witchcraft thinking is social thinking; the man examines his relationship with other people; and the diagnosis and treatment are also largely in social terms. Without going into questions of the foundations of these beliefs, it may be apparent that in the social context I have outlined, such an attitude to ill-health comes very close to our Western concept of social medicine. It is *medically* speaking very near the mark.

In Pholela, for example, we found a great deal of ill-health among the women; the prevalence of anxiety states and neurotic syndromes associated with poor nutrition and fatigue was striking. We have to consider the way they live, and in particular the basis of their married life.

Not only are women the main providers of food for their children, but because of the absence of so many men from their homes they have to make important decisions without the guidance or help of their menfolk. In no less than 55% of homes studied women were the only adults in the home for many months of the year and, while they might rely on elder kinsmen of their husbands in times of major crisis, they were in effect the key persons in the direction and management of the day-to-day affairs of the home.

This responsibility of women is a new situation in tribal terms, and the difficulty is that they have not the social status which grants them a corresponding power and authority. This is particularly true of the married women whose children are still minors. Older women, whether widowed or not, are in a somewhat different position; many live with a married son and the relationship of mother to son gives to the woman much higher status than that of a young wife to her husband. But the younger women are not expected to make decisions, and when they do, as in their husbands' absence they must, it is as likely as not that their husbands will later countermand or change their plan.

Both men and women at Pholela marry many years after puberty. Their adolescence might thus provide the opportunity for developing friendships with the other sex before final choice of a marriage partner. But such relationships are limited by the very short time that young men spend at home, and in the period of betrothal and engagement before marriage there is similarly little chance of a developing bond of affection between the couple. For the greatest part of the betrothal period the man is away at work and often only returns home shortly before the marriage.

So married life often starts with the husband and wife knowing very little of each other, either then or for a number of years thereafter. Few features of family practice impress the doctor and clinical observer more than the relative shallowness of the relationship between young married people, and the lack of adjustment between them. The young bride, as I said, is usually brought into the house of her husband's family where she lives with her in-laws while her newly-wedded husband returns to town to work. If her husband's mother is alive it is she who assumes the position of control over the bride. This relationship between the wife and mother-in-law might make life in that home very difficult, though it is true on the other hand that the mother-in-law often plays a valuable part in sorting out the frequent disagreements which arise between the young wife and her husband. Many such disagreements arise from the fact that the wife becomes aware of her husband's infidelity. Her own relations with him become disturbed, and in some cases completely ruptured. In these situations the mother often sides with her son's wife and brings pressure to bear on him so that the marriage should continue, and above all that children should be born.

It is only in old age that a woman finds life a little easier and tension decreases to some extent. She is now seldom frustrated and receives the respect of the men, especially her sons, their wives and her grandchildren. Her relationships with her own husband have also become more equable and deep affection and friendship may be found between elderly couples. Not only have they mellowed with age, but they have at long last had

the opportunity of living together for prolonged period
without the husband's continuous movement to and from th
towns.

The life of women therefore, from puberty to comparativel
old age, involves a number of frustrations. Frustration in he
sex and love life is perhaps the most important of these
commencing as it does in adolescence and proceeding throug
married life. Her relationship with her children is mor
satisfactory and the mother-child pattern of love and affectio
is very marked. But only those who have a resilient and well
developed personality are able to stand the strain imposed upo
their own self-esteem. They have to accept a position o
inferiority, which in itself need not be difficult in a society i
which girls are brought up to be submissive, but is so becaus
despite this inferior status they often have to bear grea
responsibilities. Conflict and indecision are often the result, an
the effect on their health is disastrous.

A further striking feature of Pholela is the high incidence o
infectious diseases. Prominent among these are tuberculosis
venereal disease, and acute respiratory and gastro-intestina
infections. Epidemiological studies have indicated that each o
these is closely related to the continuous movement of men t
and from the towns. The movement of large populations i
always associated with the spread of infectious disease unles
due precautions are taken. They are not taken. A way of lif
which may be sanitary for a community living within
relatively closed tribal society, is no longer sanitary when it
framework is no longer wholly tribal, and so far from bein
closed is opened by continuous inward and outward migratio
to urban slums and compounds.

Pholela is typical of many African communities. Thei
integration within the framework of industrial society is takin
place at considerable cost to the health of the present generatio

nd of future generations. The present processes of maladjustment and malnutrition can, I believe, be profoundly modified
by an extension of educationally orientated health services, and
he development of a practice of social medicine, consistent
with the needs of the people of Africa. For this, medical science
must turn increasingly to the researches of sociologists and
anthropologists for guidance, because without it we appear so
much of the time to be attending only to symptoms.

4

THE ABILITIES OF AFRICANS

by Simon Biesheuvel

The opinion is widely held, especially among European
living in Africa, that there are differences in intellectual abilit
between Africans and themselves. They generally agree tha
there are some Africans who surpass many whites in respect o
learning ability, competence in skilled or intellectual tasks, an
ability to grasp the principles underlying particular practices
but they hold that there is a much smaller proportion wit
these abilities in African groups, even when full allowance ha
been made for the Africans' limited opportunities to develop
civilization of their own and their slowness to respond t
contacts with other civilizations that did from time to tim
occur.

To these arguments the reply has been made that menta
abilities are as much a product of culture as of genetic constitu
tion, and that on the whole, environmental circumstances i
Africa have been adverse for the development of qualitie
considered valuable by Western civilization. It is claimed tha
there are sufficient grounds for believing that if environmenta
influences, in particular cultural influences, could be hel
constant, no intellectual differences between ethnic group
would remain.

I would like to consider the scientific evidence in support o
this view, both as a general proposition and as it applies t
African peoples. For the purpose of the argument, I sha

define intelligence as the capacity to gain insight into the nature of things and events, to grasp causal relations, to profit by experience and so to acquire a number of skills whereby the adjustment between individual and environment is mediated. Although this capacity, which can be looked upon as the power of the mind, is innate and genetically determined, the extent to which it is realized, the degree to which it can be effectively applied, depends on how well its growth is stimulated during the years from birth to maturity. This applies also to the type of skill that is developed, which depends largely on the needs of the culture in which the child grows up. In the origin of these skills some genetic influences must also be recognized, for it is a well-known fact that within the same culture, people differ in their capacity to use their hands and eyes, words and numbers. These differences persist despite intensive training.

It is never an easy matter to disentangle the innate and acquired components in any observed differences between people, even within the same ethnic group. Contrary to popular belief, intelligence tests do not measure innate capacity; they merely measure the effectiveness of certain skills through which the power of the mind is most readily expressed. Differences in the aggregate measures obtained from person to person are only, then, an indication of differences in innate ability if all environmental influences that have shaped the growth of the skills involved in the test were strictly comparable. This is not a condition that can readily be achieved outside a laboratory, and our knowledge concerning the share of nature and nurture in the differences that can be observed between the minds of men is still incomplete. So far, it has been possible to find out which factors are relevant; but an accurate estimate of the magnitude and permanence of their effects has not yet been made.

There is now general agreement that the most powerful

factors operate in the domestic environment. Parental interest and solicitude, affectionate care by members of the household, diversity of material objects to handle and with which to experiment; at a later stage, the intelligence, education and vocabulary of the parents and the cultural quality of the home, all these combine to provide the necessary stimulation to growth, and the soil and atmosphere in which the growing mind can thrive.

Recently, an indication has also been provided that the nutritional condition of the mother during pregnancy and the nursing period can have a measurable effect on the intelligence of her offspring. In this investigation, reported by Professor Arthur Gates of Columbia University, tablets containing either certain combinations of vitamins or an inert substance were administered to two groups of 1,200 women, attending respectively a maternity clinic in Norfolk (a coastal town in Virginia) and one in a rural area in Kentucky. In the Virginia group, who were all needy tenement dwellers, 80% Negro, the children of the mothers who had received the vitamins, when tested at three or four years, were found to have a significantly higher I.Q. than those of the mothers who had received the inert substance. The difference was as much as eight I.Q. points for those where the vitamin B complex had been supplied. In the Kentucky mountain group, on the other hand, consisting of white descendants of old Western European immigrant stock who derived a balanced diet from their cottage gardens, there was no difference between the average I.Q. of the children whose mothers had had the benefit of the vitamin treatment and those who had not.

Another environmental factor that has to be reckoned with is the general cultural, as distinct from the familial, environment. There is a tendency for children reared in a rural environment to score lower in power tests of intelligence, probably again because of the less diverse and intense stimulation they receive during the most formative years. Finally there is the effect of scholastic education, particularly important in stimulating development during the later years of childhood, and in establishing verbal, numerical and reasoning skills, without which the power of the mind can never realize its maximum potential.

Attempts have been made to assess the range of environmental variation that could be brought about by all these influences together on the deployment of innate intellectual capacity. American studies on identical twins suggest that the maximum range is approximately 40 I.Q. points, but that influences sufficiently powerful to bring about such variation occur only about once in a thousand American homes. This means that an individual with perfectly average endowment and who under average environmental conditions would have attained I.Q. 100 might once in a thousand cases strike either such favourable conditions that the power of his mind developed to I.Q. 120, which ranks as superior, or such adverse conditions that it was depressed to I.Q. 80, which ranks as subnormal. The difference is of vital importance, particularly when one considers that conditions that are extreme within a white group may be far more general in African communities.

It is difficult to generalize concerning the environmental conditions that have moulded intellectual growth in Africa, for they vary considerably from one African community to another, and within the same community according to the closeness of contact with Western civilization. We are interested, however, in those factors in respect of which there are characteristic differences between life in the West and in Africa – particularly tribal Africa, which still includes the majority of the population and which will continue to make its influence felt for many generations to come.

Neither the domestic environment, nor tribal culture and social life provide the kind of stimulation that is necessary for the adequate deployment of intelligence. Particularly for the infant, but also for the growing child, the material environment offers little scope for the development of manipulative and perceptual habits. ' Consider the fewness of toys, clothes, furniture, household utensils, the simplicty of the daily round of the tasks to be performed and the situations to be dealt with. In pre-literate cultures this simplicity extends to the mental life, where symbolic activity is virtually limited to speech. In societies governed by custom, in which only elementary cause and effect relations, often of a purely subjective kind, are appreciated, there is little to stimulate and much to inhibit thought. Curiosity is rare and the spirit of enquiry is not encouraged because there is a traditional answer for most things and magical forces provide for anything that is not understood. Maternal interest and affection, which have been found so important in creating the right atmosphere for intellectual growth, are intense during the first two years of life; but after weaning, which generally takes place in a traumatic manner, there is often separation from the parents or in any case a marked falling off in attention. The parents have little to give beyond exhorting compliance with custom and tabu, and this is particularly noteworthy in those cases where the children are receiving scholastic education, but can obtain no guidance, or reinforcement of what they have learned, from the home.

' Recent research work in Dakar, Kampala and Johannesburg, in which use was made of Gesell and similar tests, showed that African babies were precocious in motor development. They were able to hold up their heads, straighten their backs, and support their weight at a much earlier age than white babies. On the other hand, there is in the South African data a suggestion of etarded visual perceptual development. In overall development, the white infants begin to forge ahead by the third year. We do not know whether there is a genetic element in this differential development or whether the African child loses its advantage when the quantity of breast-milk falls off and it is placed on an inappropriate diet; when the need for physical care, which the mother can give, begins to yield to the need for mental stimulation in respect of which both she and the cultural environment become more and more inadequate.

Just as important as cultural influences are the effects of inadequate diet and of tropical diseases. Infantile malnutrition is endemic in the whole of Africa south of the Sahara, and numerous African children everywhere develop deficiency diseases in an acute or subclinical form. Of these, by far the most devastating is the disease known as *kwashiorkor*, a name which refers to the discoloration of the hair which is one of the symptoms. It is probably caused by severe lack of protein, complicated by vitamin deficiencies, and until recently it contributed greatly to a high infantile mortality rate. There is some evidence that the disease impairs the function of the central nervous system, and research is in progress to determine these effects more precisely by means of electroencephalography, the recording of the bio-electrical activity of the brain. The electroencephalogram is a useful means of detecting brain damage and functional neural disturbances. This type of malnutrition, even when it is not severe enough to lead to a disease, may deprive the nervous system of the substances which it needs to develop fully, and any retardation in this most formative stage may never be made good; and so there is a strong probability that the kind of nutritional depression of intelligence that was postulated in Gates's vitamin experiments in the U.S.A. is pretty general in Africa and that, if anything, its effects would be more severe.

Little is known about the extent to which other tropical diseases, such as malaria, bilharzia and hookworm, impair ability. By causing debility, they are likely to affect the vigour and liveliness of the mind, rather than its capacity, but the problem has hardly been touched by research.

Finally there is the handicap suffered by African intelligence in being largely without the benefits of formal education. Scholastic education is the mechanism which establishes the mental skills through which intelligence can best make itself effective, and whereby the mind is raised to higher adaptive levels. Though educational facilities are increasing, they as yet only touch a minority of Africans in the continent as a whole. Schooling is often confined to establishing the rudiments of literacy and arithmetic, and its effects in stimulating the mind to enquire, to criticize and to seek objective causal relations is negligible in all but the smallest minority of cases.

And yet we cannot conclude from this that if all environmental inequalities were removed, the intellectual differences between Africans and persons of European descent would be found to have vanished. In practice such differences can never be wholly removed, for Africa can never be Europe, neither climatically nor culturally. But even in laboratory experiments it is difficult, if not impossible, to establish comparable conditions. To begin with, there is no common measuring device. An intelligence test can only measure intelligence indirectly, through the medium of mental skills that vary from culture to culture. The co-called 'culture-free' intelligence tests are a misnomer. They avoid the use of verbal symbols – thereby imposing a handicap on Africans whose language ability is generally well developed – but they assume facility in the interpretation of pictorial symbols and in the use of pencil and paper, which most Africans do not possess. Performance also depends on a process of logical reasoning which requires verbal concepts that are not characteristic of African languages. Comparisons between the black and the white races based on these and other tests are therefore not valid. On the rare occasions that groups can be compared who are equally at home in Western culture and who are equally well educated, one is dealing inevitably with non-representative samples of the respective populations and no general conclusions can be drawn. 'Experiments on Negroes in the United States have shown that with improvement in environmental conditions, there is an improvement in test performance, but the critical experiment in which all conditions are equated, including attitudes, community status and the sampling factor, has yet to be performed.

The question regarding the abilities of Africans must therefore remain an open one. The possibility cannot be ignored that natural selection and isolation have produced strains in Africa that are different, both in respect of the power of the mind, and of the skills that are most readily developed.

The South African National Institute for Personnel Research has embarked on a number of long-term research programmes to throw light on these complex and vitally important questions. It has devised a method of applying tests whereby use is made of a silent cine-film to explain what the candidate has to do. Comparable data can thus be obtained from any African area, regardless of language differences. It is the intention to determine the effect of a variety of environmental and cultural influences on test performance, and in particular to find out how far mental efficiency, as measured by tests, can be improved by changes in nutrition, health, education and cultural circumstances. One of the most comprehensive studies, in which psychologists, sociologists, medical scientists and nutritional experts are collaborating, concerns the effects of sociological background, domestic environment, parental outlook and pre- and post-natal feeding on mental and physical growth. Other studies are concerned with both the constitutional and cultural determinants of personality development, for the intellectual effectiveness of Africans is not merely a matter of ability. Activity level, motivation, tempo, and character qualities must also be taken into account. Extensive practical use is already being made in the Union of South Africa of the results of some of these studies, particularly in the field of personnel selection, where it is important that optimum use should be made of the opportunities to advance that are now becoming available to Africans.

It is in this direction that research should be developed, rather than in attempting to make comparisons between races under conditions that are meaningless in relation to the realities of Africa. Meanwhile, categorical statements that are made concerning the abilities of Africans are based more on the prevailing ideologies of the twentieth century than on its record of scientific fact.

5

MIGRANT LABOUR

by D. Hobart Houghton

Migrations of workers in response to economic forces occur in most countries, but labour migrations in contemporary Africa have assumed immense proportions and have incalculable social and economic consequences. This system is the background against which nearly all aspects of contemporary Africa must be considered. Indeed many of the contributions to this book have in their different fields taken it into account. It affects not only the workers concerned but the whole of the rest of the country, black and white, urban and rural, present and – as our legislation has it – future. Furthermore it is not, of course, a system confined to the Union, but has arisen throughout the continent wherever foreign enterprise and investment and new contact with world markets have drawn Africans out of their primitive subsistence economies.

First in time, Kimberley, first in size, the Witwatersrand; other industrial centres like Durban and Cape Town in South Africa; Bulawayo, Salisbury and the Copper Belt in Rhodesia; Katanga in the Congo; Lagos, Accra and the gold mines of West Africa – all act like magnets, drawing Africans from their primitive societies. It is not only mining and industry which has this effect, for commercialized agriculture such as cocoa, tobacco, coffee and cotton, also draws labour in response to wage payments; and, though the transfer to a Rhodesian tobacco farm is not as great as that to a deep-level gold mine,

the disruptive effect upon the traditional subsistence econom
is nevertheless severe.

Two facts must be kept in mind. The first is that these labou
migrations are entirely voluntary: the men go out to work c
their own free will and are not conscripted or forced labou
The second is that though there may be subsidiary reasons, it
primarily poverty which drives them out. The low productivit
of the subsistence economies makes it difficult to satisfy even th
traditional needs, let alone provide for the new wants that hav
arisen from contact with the higher living standards of th
civilized world.

Emigrants from the traditional tribal societies would seem t
fall into three categories which I call the *emigrant breadwinner*
the *emigrant families* and the *absconders*. The emigrant breac
winners go to the towns as individuals, leaving their famili
behind in their native villages. They hope to earn enough bot
to keep themselves and to provide a surplus with which t
support their families at home. This they send back as period
remittances or take home with them on their return. Th
system has the advantage that the family group remai
relatively undisturbed. It continues to live in its home villag
children are brought up in the traditional rural environmer
and, in fact, the family is sheltered from most of the effects
the impact of an entirely new civilization.

In the case of the emigrant family the man takes his wife ar
children with him and thus avoids the disruption of family lit
but it has other disadvantages, for urban conditions may lea
much to be desired. Overcrowding, slums and an unfamili
environment may be highly repugnant to an African tribe
man. I have often heard African men say that the city is a go
place in which to earn money but no place to which to bring
wife and children, and even the boldest might well be deterr
by the slums of Lagos or Johannesburg. Generally speakin

however, when a man takes his family to town with him he is less likely to return to his native village than when he goes alone, and more likely to become part of the settled urban population.

The absconders are men and women who find the economic and social obligations imposed upon them by kinship ties and tribal tradition so burdensome that they go to town to escape. Absconding is to be found throughout the continent. The absconder cuts himself off from his family and does not send back money to assist those who remain behind, but makes a new life for himself in the city. For young men and women the temptation to abscond is strong. Why, they ask, should they continue to pay all their earnings over to their parents when escape is so easy? It is difficult for members of an individualistic society to realize how burdensome the kinship and family obligations of tribal society can be, but there are cases where even professional men have been forced to seek employment away from their home neighbourhood, for if they were to remain there, they would be overwhelmed by their relatives seeking to share their wealth.

Of course, emigrant breadwinners may stay longer in the towns and eventually send for the families to join them; migrant families may spend many years in town but eventually return to their tribal home when old; or parents may send their children back from the cities to be cared for by relatives in the rural areas from which they originally migrated. The categories are not hard and fast. Nor is it possible any longer to divide Africans into two broad classes: the Westernized, de-tribalized, urban, who have been drawn into the orbit of the world economy, and those who still belong essentially to the traditional tribal way of life. There are infinite gradations between the two extremes, and – a thing which is difficult for those outside Africa to comprehend – there are millions of Africans who not merely lie somewhere between these extremes but who spend their lives *alternating* between the tribal world and the modern industrial world. These are the emigrant bread-winners, who move to and fro between the village where they were born and the industrial centre where they earn their livelihood. At home they are primitive agriculturalists or pastoralists conforming to the traditional economic practice and living in the social environment of their tribe; in the cities they are part of a modern industrial proletariat. These are the real migratory workers.

It has been estimated that in tropical and southern Africa there are some five million of these, but accurate figures are unobtainable. There are those who cross international frontiers, such as the 330,000 who come from French territories into the Gold Coast, Senegal and Gambia, the 420,000 temporary immigrants into the Union of South Africa, or the 440,000 immigrants recorded in the 1948 census of Buganda; but these are only a small part of this mass of moving humanity. There are also the huge migrations which take place within some of the territories, such as 500,000 domiciled in the Reserves of the Union who are away working in the cities, or the thousands from the Northern Province who work in the south of Ghana. Another difficulty arises because periodic censuses tell us only where a person is on census day. It is estimated that 50% of the able-bodied men are away from the Transkei at any given time. This might be misinterpreted to mean that only 50% of the Transkei males are migrant workers whereas in reality practially all the adult males are migrant workers of whom half are away at any time. When these return their places are taken by the other half.

I would like to illustrate the life of a migrant worker by an actual case, one of the many I recorded in Keiskammahoek, Native Reserve in the south-eastern part of South Africa where I conducted an economic survey in 1949.

This man was born in 1892. He went to school, but only reached Standard I (which is just above the kindergarten level). He first went out to work for the German West African Railways (1,200 miles from home) in 1908 when he was 16. After 13 months he came home for 2 years during which time he underwent the initiation ceremony into manhood. Then to work at the Premier Mine, Pretoria (730 miles away) for 8 months. Then home for 8 months. Then to the Witwatersrand (700 miles away) for 9 months as a mine worker. Then home again. Then back to the Witwatersrand where he worked as a miner for 3 years. Then home again for 7 months. Back to the Witwatersrand for 9 months. Then home again. Back to the mines again for 2 years. In November 1919 he came home. During this period he was married and was given a piece of land in the village by the chief for his wife to cultivate. But in February 1921 he was off again, this time to Cape Town (826 miles away) where he found work as a domestic servant in a convent. He was away 6 months. Then home again for the birth of his first son. Then back to Cape Town to work for a building contractor. Then home again. Back again to Cape Town, this time to be a dairy delivery boy. Then home again. Next time he went off it was to work in a steel works in Benoni, in the Transvaal. Thence to an electric plating works in Johannesburg, where he worked for a year, and then he went into domestic service in Johannesburg. In all he was away this time for $4\frac{1}{2}$ years. Then home again, a long visit of over 4 years. Then back to the gold mines for 13 months. Then home again. After 3 further spells of work on the mines he returned home in 1945 and said he did not intend to go out to work again. He had five sons, one of whom died in infancy, and two of whom were away working in Cape Town and Johannesburg at the time of the survey. They had all received several more years of schooling than he had. His wife was still alive, but was away working in a neighbouring town at the time of the survey.

What strikes one is the length of working life as a migrant worker (from the age of 16 to 53), and the variety of employment he has had (16 different jobs in 5 large cities). But apart from that he is in no way unusual: he is just one of the 1,000,000 adult males domiciled in the Reserves of the Union of whom about 487,000 are away working at any given moment.

The social consequences of migrant labour, both in the industrial centres and in the traditional tribal societies from which they emigrate, are examined by other speakers. As an economist, the first point that I should like to raise is that the migratory system is economically inefficient, not merely because of the enormous cost of transporting the workers to and fro, which represents a charge against the net product of labour which must necessarily depress wages, but also because it condemns the workers in perpetuity to undifferentiated unskilled labour. The intermittent character of their employment prevents the acquisition of skill, and the periodic visits home give rise to a high labour turn-over. The mining companies have succeeded in accommodating themselves to the system, but the growth of manufacturing shows up the low productivity and the ineptitude of the migrant worker most clearly. The manager of a textile factory said to me recently 'African labour as such is good, but the labour turn-over is terrible. In Lancashire we expect to have to train 3% to 4% of our workers per annum: here it is about 60%.' A recent study in a rubber factory in Durban reveals that the productivity of unselected African migrant labour is only 29% of that of normal white workers in continuous employment, but that the productivity of African labour can be raised to 85% if they are selected and in continuous employment. The report states: 'The migratory nature of Native labour is thus seen to be the most important cause of the low productivity.'[1]

At the rural end the migratory system also has evil consequences. In the Keiskammahoek district about half the able-bodied men were away, and a considerable proportion of the women as well, with the result that the already low yield from subsistence agriculture was declining still further, for the migrants represent the most active workers. Productivity was so low that the population was wholly unable to support itself from farming activities and was dependent upon imports for all clothing and manufactured goods and about half its food. Apart from the export of a little wool, these were paid for by the export of labour. Remittances from emigrant workers in the cities provided almost 50% of the total cash income and without this the population of the district would have starved.

Migrant labour may be regarded as a temporary phenomenon resulting from the impact of a highly developed civilization upon a primitive culture; but it has shown itself to be very persistent. It has been going on in South Africa for nearly three-quarters of a century and although the number of permanently urbanized Africans has increased vastly, the number of regular migrants has shown no tendency to decline. There is no easy solution to the problem, for the mines and industries depend largely upon migrant workers for their labour and the rural areas could not survive without the incomes earned by the emigrants. It can only end when the families of the urban workers have moved to town and taken up their permanent abode there, but this involves moving millions, and apart from the physical problems of transport, housing, sanitation, and urban services there are deep-seated prejudices and sometimes legal obstacles to be overcome. The

[1] *The African Factory Worker:* see Reading List.

adaptation to urban conditions is difficult, necessitating th abandonment of many tribal customs and traditions.

The migratory system is likely to persist for a long time t come but it should be recognized as a very imperfect adapta tion to the impact of the world upon the primitive subsistenc economies of Africa. A computation of the number of man years spent by Africans in travelling to and fro would revea deplorable waste of manpower in a desperately poor continen but the most serious and tragic consequences are not th economic but the psychological and spiritual consequences c being perpetually on the move. Uprootedness and the lack of feeling of belonging anywhere is the greatest curse of Afric today, and is the fundamental background to crime i Johannesburg, strikes on the Copperbelt, and to Mau Mau The cost of a temporary relief from poverty is the separation o husbands from wives and fathers from children for the greate part of their lives, and in this way migrant labour destroys th foundations of the traditional tribal society while at the sam time it inhibits the growth of full new community life in th urban areas.

6

THE GROWTH OF TOWNS
(Northern Rhodesia)

by J. Clyde Mitchell

The slave trade from the centre to the east coast of Africa came to an abrupt end when the British South Africa Company extended its activities northwards across the Zambesi. The last slave caravan was intercepted in 1903. The trade was not only inhuman and immoral. From the point of view of the authorities it constituted an iniquitous abduction of valuable labour. As Mr Lewis Gann has put it: 'The slave trade was the original form of labour migration in Africa. Before it could be suppressed the new form of labour migration enforced by the signed contract and the tax receipt, instead of the slaver's musket, could not come into existence.'

But the end of the slave trade did not mean that the Africans came tumbling out of their villages into the white man's cities. A tribal system has a certain tenacity of its own. It is not easy to prise a man out of it, and it was some time before the tribes of Northern Rhodesia took to the idea of labour migration. The authorities found it difficult to tip the decanter initially: they find it equally difficult to stem the flow today.

Recent estimates put the African population of the Copper-belt at approximately 200,000. The men employed on the mines, and their families, all live in the African townships erected by the mines. Most of those employed outside the mines, that is by commerce, government and building

contractors, as well as many domestic servants, live in th
townships or suburbs erected and maintained by the loca
authorities. These are not townships in the sense that they ar
administratively and financially autonomous groups within th
precincts of the industrial area. They are essentially residentia
areas administered directly by the mining companies for thei
employees, or by the municipal councils through paid Euro
pean and African officials for the employees of its ratepayer:
The finances for the maintenance of the areas come out of th
company funds or the general revenue of the municipality. Th
administrative centre of the township is the office of the Africa
personnel manager on the mines, or his counterpart, th
Director of African Administration, in the municipalities. Th
social centre is the welfare hall where entertainments or publi
meetings take place. A local market and a few shops usuall
supply the daily needs of the people though the main spendin
is done in the so-called 'second class trading areas' in the publi
townships, outside the African areas. The houses, nowadays
are usually two-, three-, four- or even five-roomed structure
with asbestos roofs, of a standard far higher than the usua
village hut. The temporary houses erected in great number
during and shortly after the last war differed little from th
village huts but the improvements since then have bee
considerable. But however fast these new houses are buil
the influx of Africans is so great that many of the older house
must still remain occupied.

The rate of expansion was not always as rapid as this, but th
1914–1918 war was a turning point. The campaign on Norther
Rhodesia's doorstep had necessitated the movement of me
and materials through areas hitherto untouched, and so brough
some of the products of Western civilization to thousands o
men and women who otherwise may not have known of the
for many years to come. Secondly, the demand for ra

materials following Europe's industrial expansion after the war awakened interest in the minerals of Northern Rhodesia which, for technical reasons, had lain untouched for 25 years.

It was in 1927 that the first shafts of the new copper mines were sunk and at that time about 11,000 Africans were employed. In two years – just before the recession set in – the number had doubled. This increase in the labour force had been achieved at no little cost of effort. Labour in those days had to be recruited and the agents operated far and wide to bring it to the mines. Many thousands of Northern Rhodesian Africans were going to Tanganyika, the Congo, and Southern Rhodesia, many of them into mining occupations. Nyasaland Africans were coming into Northern Rhodesia to agricultural occupations. But recruiters found it difficult to find labourers who would come to the copper mines – so much so that in 1929 a large number of 'alien natives' were recruited in Southern Rhodesia to work in the Northern mines.

It is not easy to account for this prejudice against the copper mines in the early stages. The conditions on them were no worse and wages no lower than elsewhere. Some Africans were prejudiced against one particular mine because they believed that a large snake lived in a nearby river and caused the death of labourers in some mysterious way. But no such rumours had developed about the other copper mines. In the lack of other information we can only conclude that the poor recruiting draw of the copper mines lay in the conservatism of the labourers and the grip of the 'old familiar things and places'.

Whatever the cause of the prejudice, it was short-lived. The world-wide economic recession began to affect Central Africa shortly afterwards and by 1931, when the depth of the depression had reached these areas, not only had the recruiting stopped but Northern Rhodesian Africans were being repatriated from the Congo. This was the end of labour supply problems

for the copper mines. From then onwards as the indust
recovered recruiting was never again necessary. In 1940 abo
29,000 Africans were employed in the copper mining industr
By the end of 1954 this number had doubled. Over the la
10 years the annual rate of increase has been slightly over 5%

The increase in other sources of wage employment ha
increased commensurately, so that the towns have been i
creasing over the last 10 years at a rate considerably higher tha
the rate of increase of the African population as a whole.
estimate that the African population of the towns of Norther
Rhodesia has been increasing at the rate of about 10% p
annum against the overall natural increase of only $2\frac{1}{2}$% p
annum.

The mechanics of the increase may appear simple enoug
more people are living in towns. But in fact the trend appea
to be the resultant of a number of somewhat complicat
demographic processes. First, there is the possibility th
because of better medical facilities in towns and because urba
populations are selected in favour of young married couple
the natural increase in the towns is greater than in the rur
areas. The demographic survey of 1950 showed that the averag
number of births per year per adult woman was higher in t
towns than in rural areas. I do not think that this is becau
women in the towns are more fertile, but because the urba
population is heavily loaded in the most fertile age groups, th
is between 20 and 29. Nevertheless the general demograph
result is that the urban areas must show a greater annu
increase of total population than the rural areas and to som
extent this must partly account for the current rapid growth o
the urban populations.

Secondly, there appears to be a steady increase of th
proportion of women and children in the towns. Not only a
there more men coming to work in towns, but more men a

inging their wives and children with them. To illustrate this
om one copper mine: in 1934 only 48% of the African men
d their families with them. By 1954, 75% had their families
ith them. A good proportion of the remaining 25% were
oung men who had never married so that the proportion who
d left their wives in the rural areas must be very small. It
llows, therefore, that as more wives and families come to town
e urban population increases more rapidly than the mere
crease of the male working population suggests.

The third factor which makes for the swelling of the Copper-
elt towns is that there may have been a change in the quantity
f migration to the towns. By this I mean that possibly a
eater proportion of potential migrants have become real
igrants. Unfortunately it is very difficult to get a measure of
is, partly because it begs the question of who the potential
igrants are, and partly because the collection of the requisite
ata is so difficult. The estimates of Administrative officers of
e proportion of tax-payers absent from their districts each
ar over the last twenty years, seem to suggest that there has
en no radical change. But a complex phenomenon such as
igration cannot be measured by a simple percentage. A
easure of the degree of labour migration must take into
count not only the number of people away, but how long
ey have been away, and whether they are likely to return
ithin any given period. The current measures of labour
igration are analogous to the crude death rate, while the
atistic we need is analogous to the life table.

A fourth demographic process which may contribute to the
owth of towns in Northern Rhodesia is the change in the
uality of migration. When an African leaves his rural village
 seek work in town for the first time, it is unlikely that he has
y doubts about his eventual return. It is not a case of his
acking up and moving into town for good. On the contrary

he feels that his home is in the village and that he will return
it some day. What in fact happens is, of course, a differe
matter. Sometimes he comes back after a while, sometimes f
a while, and sometimes he never comes back at all and becom
what the villagers sadly call a *muchona* – a lost one. It follo
that if for some reason the average length of stay of an Afric
in town increases, for a period at any rate, the total populatic
of the town will also show an increase. People are coming in
town at the same rate but they are not leaving it so quickly. I
due course when the period of stay is stabilized then this sort
artificial growth of the town will cease.

Whether towns will continue to grow at the present ra
depends on the extent to which their economic bases rema
stable. At the moment there are very few Africans in the tow
over the age of 50 – after all the towns only came into bei
25 years ago. The extent to which they will stay in town
their old age depends on whether they can find employme
suitable for old people, or some other kind of financial suppor
or, conversely, on whether the tribal systems in their rur
homes have changed so much that they have nowhere else to g

These are not yet serious problems – they will begin t
appear in the next ten years when the men who were prese
at the sinking of the first shafts and who have stayed in tow
ever since, find themselves too old to go on working. Th
mining companies have foreseen this problem and hav
introduced a pension scheme for their older African employee
But a pension scheme in itself does not solve the problem. Th
retired African worker must be able to retire to a *home* and th
question is: where is that home to be? In the rural areas whic
he left when he was a young man and has scarcely revisite
since? Or in the towns where, as yet, there are few opportur
ities for Africans to acquire fixed property?

In the meantime the ceaseless flow of people to and from tl

opperbelt goes on. No longer are they fettered in slave-sticks
ıd chains and driven by the whip of the caravan master.
ıstead they obey a far more exacting and compelling master.
. slave could always hope that a kinsman of his might offer a
ısk of ivory and so redeem him, or with luck he could escape
om the plantation on the east coast.

But from the grip of Western money economy there is no
scape.

7

LABOUR MIGRATION AND THE TRIBE
(Northern Rhodesia)

by J. Clyde Mitchell

How many able-bodied men can you take out of a communi
without causing a general social and economic degeneration
This is a problem which has often crossed the minds of Distri
Commissioners in Northern Rhodesia and Nyasaland, wher
according to their reports, as many as 75% of the tax-paye
are away from their rural villages at any one time working i
the mines or towns.

It is obvious that there is no single answer to the question.
depends on the part that men play in growing the food and
running the particular tribal system. There are many differe
sorts of tribal system in Northern Rhodesia and Nyasaland, b
not all of them have been studied in sufficient detail to enab
us to draw valid conclusions from them. I think, however, th
we can select three which have been studied sufficiently well t
illustrate what I mean.

One of the clearest examples we have are the Bemba
Northern Rhodesia, studied by Dr Audrey Richards betwee
1933 and 1935. The Bemba live in the Northern Province
Northern Rhodesia where the soil is generally poor. The
staple item of food is millet which they grow by sowin
the seeds in patches of ash left after the branches of the su
rounding trees have been lopped off, dragged into the centre
a clearing and burnt. In Bemba country, unlike other parts

e territory, the trees are not cut down at shoulder height. stead the young men with some daring and not a little avado climb some 20 or 30 feet up into the trees and lop the anches off at that height. The women and children then rry the branches into the centre of the garden. A newly made rden yields a good crop for the first year, but the plant trients contained in the ash are soon used up, so that a new tch of trees must be pollarded each year to provide enough od to last the year through. So the village gardens gradually t their way into the bush further and further away from the llage. Periodically, about every five years, the village must root itself and find a new site nearer the gardens. Eventually, ter about 25 years the trees that were originally pollarded ve grown again and the village can return to its old site.

It follows from this that given this type of slash-and-burn ltivation, there is a direct relationship between the density of e population on the land, and the period of regeneration that e land will be allowed. If the population goes up too rapidly gger gardens must be cut and the village comes round to its st site before the full regeneration of the natural growth on it. this happens the land may become over-cultivated so that the il degenerates and the yields fall, with a resulting depression the standard of living of the villagers.

The population carrying capacity of the land has been died particularly by William Allen, an agriculturalist orking in Northern Rhodesia. Allen says: 'Any given area of nd will maintain in perpetuity a limited number of people d this limit is determined by certain natural characteristics of e soil and climate, and by the manner in which the land used.' This limit he calls the critical density. The critical nsity among some people who use relatively advanced agri-ltural methods is as high as 120 persons per square mile. mong the Ngoni, Chewa, Nsenga and Lamba, who practice a

type of agricultural technique involving soil selection, it is abo
22. Among the Swaka, who practice a type of slash-and-bu
agricultural technique, it is about 12. Among the Bisa an
Eastern Lala, whose slash-and-burn agriculture is not as efficien
as the Bemba's, the critical density is only 5. Among the Bemb
themselves, it is probably not very much higher than this – sa
7 or 8. This means to say that the Bemba country will be ove
populated if the density increases much above this. It show
what a small margin there is between the Bemba and starvatio

The Bemba have only the simplest of implements to wor
with – the hoe and the axe. It is strenuous work to cut dow
trees: it is essentially the work of men. To cut the branches o
trees perched some twenty feet above the ground is not onl
work for men – it is work for *young* men.

It happens that the Bemba area supplies most of the men t
the Copperbelt. In December 1954 no less than 43% of th
total labour force on the Copperbelt came from the Norther
Province, including the two Luapula valley districts.

It is easy to see that the absence of men, especially the youn
men, constitutes a severe blow to the indigenous method o
agriculture among the Bemba. The few men left in the rur
areas are unable to cut enough new gardens for the women an
the very old who are left behind, who must continue to culti
vate the same plots of ground over and over again, and so th
yields fall rapidly. As long ago as 1938 the late Godfrey Wilso
had described Bembaland as the 'hungry, manless area'. H
description is even more true today. Dr Richards's study mad
it very clear that the Bemba live constantly on the verge o
starvation: they have no surplus food stores to fall back o
They *expect* to go hungry every year as their last year's foo
supplies give out and before the new crops are harvested. He
studies show that over the whole year the average intake o
calories per man value is only 1,700. Mrs Thomson who mad

tudy amongst the Lala, who have a similar system of agri-
lture, found the average intake per man value to be 2,000.
e also made a study in an urban area, and found that the
erage calorific intake per man value was nearly twice as much
in the rural areas.

In the Bemba areas, and in areas like them where men play
indispensable part in food production, the effect of the drift
town is to set up a sort of circular action. The absence of the
en lowers the standard of living in the rural areas and this in
rn tends to encourage more of the able bodied to leave the
ral areas to seek a higher standard of living in the towns. The
tistics show this quite clearly. The number of people from
e Northern Province on the Copperbelt has been increasing
just less than double the rate of the natural increase in the
ral areas. In contrast the number of men from the Luapula
as, where an alternative source of cash income – and food –
available in the form of fish, has increased at 3% per annum
ich is only slightly above the average rate of natural increase.

The northern neighbours of the Bemba are the Mambwe.
Watson of the Rhodes-Livingstone Institute has made an
ensive study of the effect of wage labour on the tribal
ucture of these people. The Mambwe in the northern part
the territory do not practise the slash-and-burn type of
ltivation. They occupy open grassland and not the woodland
at the Bemba do. In order to grow their staple crop, eleusine,
ey turn the grass into the centre of mounds and this rots to
rm a bed rich in humus. This sort of agriculture is not the
ork of men to the same degree that the pollarding of trees
among the Bemba. The result is that men may be away from
e Mambwe country and yet not affect the level of food
oduction seriously. The Mambwe thus operate a sort of
vision of labour, which is intimately related to the kinship
ucture of their communities. Some of the men are away in

the towns earning money while others at home are supportin
themselves on the land. The men in the towns retain a stake i
the land at home and when they come back they share tl
wealth they have earned with those who stayed at home.

Hence in a society with this type of agricultural productic
many more men can be away without upsetting the econom
life of the tribe than is possible with the Bemba. Dr Watso
suggests that the limit to the number of men who can be awa
is reached where there are two women to each man left in tl
villages, and this limit has not yet been reached.

The Tonga who live up the western coast of Lake Nya:
provide an extreme variation of the same pattern. Mr va
Velsen, also of the Rhodes-Livingstone Institute, has describe
how as many as 75% of the Tonga men may be away at o1
time, most of them in South Africa and Southern Rhodesia. Y
he was impressed by the comparative affluence of the Tong
Many of them wore good clothing and had good houses. H
found that few of them were interested in earning wag
locally. The staple food among the Tonga is cassava or manic
which is propagated by planting slips of the stem in mound
into which the grass and weeds have been turned. The edib
roots of the plant then develop in the rich soil which resul
from the rotting vegetation within the mound. There a
various types of cassava, some of which mature in six montl
and others which may remain in the ground for as long :
two years. Among the Tonga, therefore, a man is able t
prepare a large garden of cassava before he goes to Sout
Africa and leave it to his wife to maintain and live off while l
is away earning money.

I think it is clear from these examples that the absence (
men does not affect each system the same way, and it is in
possible to lay down a hard-and-fast rule about the number (
men who may leave a tribe without causing disorganization.

It seems to me, therefore, that the breakdown of the tribal system is less likely to arise from the mere absence of men – to which, within limits, the tribal system can adjust itself – than from the development of classes of Africans who did not exist in the tribal system before.

The policy makers in Northern Rhodesia appreciate very keenly the danger of allowing large towns to develop on the basis of such wasting assets as copper and cobalt on the Copperbelt and lead and zinc at Broken Hill. They also appreciate that even the towns that now exist need food to keep them going. Until recently, insufficient maize was grown within the territory to keep those towns supplied, and most of the maize that was offered for sale was grown by European farmers. The necessity for agricultural development among the Africans is obvious.

The Northern Rhodesia Government has been attempting to stimulate this in many ways. In the 'Improved Farmers Scheme' each African who farms his land according to improved practices is paid a bonus for each acre of land so cultivated. The 'Peasant Farmers Scheme' makes provision for the individual tenure of land in certain parts of the territory, one of the conditions of tenure being that the farmer should adopt improved methods. Largely as a result of these measures, for the first time in many years Northern Rhodesia produces enough maize at least to feed itself.

The problem of increased agricultural production no doubt can be solved technically – it is a question of experimentation with different fertilizers and systems of crop rotation and so on. There are however certain social repercussions of these schemes that should be considered. Modern farming methods involve the investment of capital in machinery and equipment and for efficient use of this machinery it must be used on fairly large holdings. A man who lives in a tribal system is bound to his

fellow tribesmen by certain rights and obligations which for
part of the social structure of the tribe. A man who reaps
bumper crop is expected to distribute the food amongst his l
fortunate kinsmen.

This exchange of goods and the distribution of weal
among kinsmen constitutes part and parcel of the trib
system. From one point of view we can regard this as
investment of surplus wealth in social security because over t
course of years today's giver will be tomorrow's receiver. B
if a man is to set himself up as a successful farmer and to inv
his surplus wealth in equipment, fertilizers, mechanical tran
port, labour and so on he must shake himself free from t
shackles of the ever-ramifying kinship system. He must be ab
to cultivate more land than traditionally a man could with
axe and hoe, and he must dispose of the surplus crops for cas
He must use this cash, over and above his immediate requir
ments, to buy seeds and repair his equipment, to pay his labo
and so on. He must therefore reject the claims of his kinsm
and turn them hungry from his door. This, of course, is not
easy thing to do. Virtually it means isolating himself fro
social relationships with his fellows and this is almost certain
evoke their hostility. It will also cost him money because
involves having at hand sufficient financial resources to me
medical costs, the costs of litigation, the costs of funerals, t
costs of old age dependency and the many other types
expenses which, in the tribal system are distributed amongs
wide group of kinsmen.

The creation of a sufficiently large class of individual farme
it seems to me, inevitably means the passing of the old trib
system as we know it. No doubt sufficient food and oth
agricultural produce will be produced to supply the urb
masses. But at the same time, from one point of view the trib
system has been supplying a hidden subsidy to industr

evelopment in Northern Rhodesia. By assuming responsi-
ility for the care of the lame and the aged who return from the
ndustrial areas, and the unproductive youths before they go
nto the industrial areas, the rural tribesmen in the past have
een bearing the costs of what otherwise would have to be
orne by government in the shape of welfare services, or by
ndustry in the form of higher wages. They have borne these
osts, of course, at the expense of their standard of living, for
he tribal system is essentially egalitarian, and tribesmen in the
ast, because of the kinship and tribal obligations, have been
repared to share what they have with their poorer fellows.
Change, it seems, is inevitable and the old tribal system must
o. But the change is going to be expensive for government
nd industry and for the Africans themselves.

8

TOWN AND TRIBE
(Southern Rhodesia)

by J. F. Holleman[1]

When we think of racial problems it is usually of the black white relationship and of the urban areas, because it is especial here that the spearhead of the new African middle-class tries forge ahead, voices grievances, and makes demands.

In our inevitable preoccupation with this aspect we tend lose sight of the rural areas where the great majority of the African population still lives, the vast reservoir of tradition African life and thought. The pace of development is slow here, and its pattern basically different. And from this emerge the problem I want to discuss: that behind the glare and in mediacy of the black-white problem, there is a growin estrangement between African and African, a steadily widenin gap which may one day surprise us with its immensity an tragedy.

Let me first give you an outline of the rural situation as found it in Mashonaland, in the eastern part of Souther Rhodesia. In the more remote areas you will still find the traditional picture, the small, impermanent clusters of low an sometimes untidy-looking thatched huts, with the picturesqu granaries like oversized mushrooms perched on low rock around this a spreading angular patchwork of fields and gar

* At the time of these broadcasts Dr Holleman was Senior Welfa Officer, Bulawayo Municipality.

lens, and beyond, the wide and often rather bare-looking *bundu*, in which the hamlets lie scattered, half a mile to a few miles from each other, seeking the shelter of granite outcrops, or crouching low under a few shady trees. Each hamlet is the home of between ten and forty people, children included, and each is a tightly knit kinship unit with a considerable measure of autonomy. But across the *bundu* innumerable ties of kinship stretch in all directions to other hamlets, where everyone seems to be a father, mother, brother, uncle, nephew or son of every-one else: a dense and intricate network of kinship relations which tie the scattered hamlets together in a wide social pattern, which is the strong and flexible basis of organized life and political authority in the area, its living reality permeating every aspect of life, work and thought.

In the agricultural season people from neighbouring villages gather in parties, men, women and children, the guests of someone who has prepared beer to attract them – partly to get a great deal of work done by many hands, partly because of the fun and satisfaction of playing host to so many relatives and friends. Almost every field-owner does this once or twice a season, and especially at times of weeding and harvesting the schedule of such parties is very tight indeed. For weeks on end the evenings are filled with the sound of drums, singing, danc-ing and laughter, which mark the end of a day's collective work in the fields. An efficiency expert may doubt the value of these parties, but in this society they are a keystone of the economic organization, and the very heart of social intercourse. Then there are the rituals, of birth, marriage, death and the festive bringing home of a deceased person's spirit; again, family affairs, in which relatives and friends from miles around participate as a matter of course and of duty.

The physical aspect of rural life in the tribal areas has changed. A government-controlled policy of agriculture and

soil conservation is now reaching even the most remote areas
and the scattered and impermanent hamlets are vanishing. It i
far more common to see bigger and more stable villages, their
brick huts and storage places laid out in a straight pattern, with
carefully pegged-out fields stretching in one direction, and
pasture lands in the other. You will find contour ridges and
furrows, crop rotation, ox-drawn ploughs and cultivators
scotchcarts, bicycles, enamel ware, wooden cupboards, table
and chairs. Clothing has become almost completely westernized – even the old women, the last to discard their skin aprons
go about in cotton dresses. The number of traditional drums i
getting smaller, and battery-charged radios are becoming a
fashionable as guitars and gramophones.

People need no longer wait for a hunt or ritual before they
can taste meat, because there are African butcheries where
cattle are killed even without the spirits requesting their
sacrifice. Thousands of pounds of cash change hands in the rural
areas, and the numerous native truck stores generally flourish
and while flourishing, they further whet the people's appetite
for more, and more varied, material possessions.

Change is apparent everywhere: in the language of the men
coming home from a spell of employment on the European
farms, in the towns and mines, in the games and songs o
children who go to school. And yet, the traditional spirit o
kinship and community is still there; the collective beer and
work parties, the public interest in the joys and sorrows of a
neighbour's life, the wide and active participation in family
rituals. Many, it is true, are now Christians, and this does affec
the attendance at rain ceremonies and similar public function
which depend for their success on the participation of *all* the
members of the community. And there are the tribal cour
sessions, under a shady tree or a sheltering rock, an odd bu
heart-warming mixture of formal codes of behaviour and

confused informality, of high civic responsibility and ribald fun – a wonderful stage on which everyone present may help to expose, with candour and clamour, the wisdom and follies of the human animal. It is still like that, although chief and assessors may now sit on chairs behind a table instead of on logs, and the clerk of the court may scribble in a foolscap register with a fountain pen.

In short, the visible aspect of rural society, its people and their way of life, have undoubtedly changed very considerably, and in a short space of time.

How profound is this change, and how far does it keep pace with modern development in African *urban* life? Some cynics say that it is merely a matter of appearance and that all this change no more than touches the skin of the rural African. Others again, and among them government planners and administrators, are convinced that the very fabric of tribal society has changed. The first view is, I think, untenable; even a switch from skin clothes to European dress, from hoe to plough, from mystically doctored seed to manure and crop rotation, cannot take place without some corresponding change in mental attitude. And when thousands upon thousands turn from shifting homesteads and shifting cultivation to controlled agriculture and residential stability, from paganism to Christianity, from illiteracy to some literacy, this must inevitably influence their outlook on life and community, the pattern of their thought and the shape of their ambitions. On the other hand, those who speak of changing the very fabric of tribal society refer to fundamental aspects and concepts. Let me therefore test their convictions and take three aspects which are pretty fundamental in any society, of whatever colour:

First: *the philosophy of life and death.*

The pagan Mashona scheme includes a vague concept of a

God-Creator (*Mwari*), but he represents something so remote
and nebulous that I have found no regular form of *Mwari*-
worship of any consequence. Far more important is the
ancestral cult. Here is a philosophy which, although not always
very articulate, does present a recognizable outline and is, above
all, of practical significance as a potent instrument for directing
(or correcting) human behaviour.

The set-up in the ancestral spirit world is very similar to that
among the living: lineal hierarchies in which the spirits of the
deceased kinsmen are ranked according to seniority and
generation. In fact, it *is* the same set-up, because each spiritual
hierarchy grows and extends into the living and physical
present and the as yet unborn future. This concept, that the
ancestral spirits are an integral part of the existing and continuously growing lineage structure, lends to the relationship
between the living, junior generations, and the spiritual,
senior generations, a general simplicity, immediacy and inti-
macy (sometimes, indeed, familiarity), which in our religion is
experienced only in moments of exaltation and by very few. It
has, moreover, a deeply personal element because, even before
birth, the spirit of a deceased grandparent enters a person's
body, staying with him through life, guiding his behaviour,
while his own personal spirit lies dormant, waiting to be
released as an independent junior spirit. When the physical
body dies, both the senior and junior spirit escape. For the
junior spirit, two conditions must be fulfilled before it is
considered to have done its share in the reproductive process of
the lineage. It must find its appropriate place in the spiritual
hierarchy; and it must, in turn, enter into a lineal grandchild.
For both steps it needs the assistance of the surviving kinsmen
and descendants. These must make the first step possible by
staging an appropriate full-scale ritual ('the bringing home of
the spirit'), and the second step, by finding daughters-in-law to

produce the grandchildren. The spirits retain some of their human characteristics; they are quick to feel neglected, hurt or offended, and are then capable of sudden and spiteful action, which may threaten life and property. This is one potent reason for the living to preserve the peace with their spiritual seniors: hence the family rituals and the fairly frequent small sacrificial tributes in meat, beer or snuff tobacco, to acknowledge the beneficial interest taken by the ancestral spirits.

This very sketchy and incomplete fragment of Shona philosophy may give an idea of the immediacy and practical impact of pagan beliefs. A large number of people, however, have been converted to Christianity, go to church and mission schools, and earnestly try to follow the Christian way of life and thinking. I have no doubt about their sincerity. But the difficulty for these people is that, compared with the immediacy and seeming reality of pagan beliefs, the concepts of Christian faith are abstract and remote. When the going is fair, there is no problem. In times of misfortune and stress, however, the Christian faith enjoins fortitude through prayer and resignation, while paganism stands ready with a simple explanation and a simple remedy. Christianity demands a sustained spiritual effort and mental discipline; paganism prescribes material sacrifice. God does not promise that misfortune shall not recur; but the pagan spirits threaten disaster if the sacrifice is not made. There are few who do not, under such pressure, reach back for the direct, simple and seemingly plausible prescriptions of their ancestral faith, often only after a desperate spiritual rear-guard action, and not rarely in the form of a face-saving device – by asking a pagan relative to apply the pagan remedy on his behalf.

Although such lapses are common, they do not mean a reconversion to paganism. Such people consider themselves erring Christians and not reconfirmed pagans.

Now the second fundamental aspect: *the basis of marriage and family*.

Under customary law a valid marriage is contracted by the families of the man and woman – not so much by the individuals themselves – after a series of formal negotiations during which certain concrete tokens or payments are made and accepted, which are legal proof of the intentions of the contracting parties. Except in extremely rare cases, only the payment of a recognized bridewealth to the woman's family establishes the right of the husband's family to the children of this marriage. This was the fundamental principle of marriage and family among the Mashona and many other tribes. It still is in present-day rural society. It has not changed merely because a considerable cash amount has taken the place of the traditional hoe as a marriage proposal token, because the father-in-law may be given a shirt instead of a calabash of snuff, because the formal love token may be a bible or comb and mirror instead of the customary bead necklace, and because sometimes, in the absence of cattle, cash or other value may be given as bridewealth. This applies also to Christian marriages in the rural areas. With a few exceptions all couples first comply with the requirements prescribed by customary law (and this includes bridewealth), before they go to church to be married by Christian rites.

The third fundamental aspect is *the concept of wealth and prosperity*.

In old Mashona society material needs were very limited, and wealth had little meaning except as a means of enhancing social and political status. But these depended largely on seniority in the kinship system and the support of a large number of kinsmen. Wealth was therefore looked upon mainly as a means of reproducing one's own blood, and a prosperous man was a man with a large and growing family. In this concept, cattle hold a key position, because cattle mean bridewealth, and bridewealth means wives and more children.

This idea of wealth, as a source of family reproduction rather than material riches, has remained surprisingly strong. In spite of the growing economic value of cattle, the great majority of cattle transactions is still for the purpose of marriage, and not for other, more economic reasons.

Western influence has introduced a host of new material values and economic ideas, and these have gained a firm foothold in tribal society. In fact, the visible evidence of the new economy is so plentiful that one may think that it has all but replaced the old standards of value. But this is deceptive. In the Chibi Reserve I found villagers growing vegetables for the European market, and selling grain to European stores. Money was plentiful. All had engaged additional labour on their fields during the season, but the total amount paid in cash for this labour, in the whole area, was less than two pounds ten shillings. All had fallen back on the traditional beer-work party when they needed help.

A man may readily accept five pounds as the equivalent of one head of cattle in a marriage transaction; a day later he may refuse to accept ten pounds from a butcher for a similar animal, hotly arguing that this is less than the market value. Here you find one mind applying two utterly different standards of value with regard to the same thing. And without being aware of a conflict. For the new economy has not so much replaced the old one, as found a place alongside it. Each functions in a sphere of its own and, so far at least, more or less isolated from the other.

If it is now asked how profoundly Western influence has changed traditional rural society, I will side-step and say that what is profound is still traditional. I certainly do not deny the very great changes that are taking place and that some of them go deep. But I cannot underrate the fact that all this takes place against the vast established background and within the existing and extremely resilient frame of traditional African society.

Herein lies the basic and inescapable difference between the changing rural scene and the new African urban scene, and the reason why they are bound to grow apart. It is the complete absence in a city like Bulawayo or Salisbury of any cohesive pattern of traditional life and organization. You do find that kinsmen seek contact with each other, but there is no kinship system, and therefore no authority based on seniority. You will still find many people who believe in ancestral spirits, but there is no ancestral cult. There are still bridewealth marriages but they are anomalies without the wider relationship between the families. You will find many scattered bits and pieces of many different tribal backgrounds, but these are useless building material for a modern urban community. And yet there is a conscious urge towards some form of internal cohesion, which expresses itself in the formation of dozens of small and not-so-small clubs and societies, each with a paper constitution and some money in the bank. In many of these there is still an element of tribal affiliation, but there is a strong modern trend away from tribalism and traditional culture. Progress and development is seen only as a struggle to follow the Western pattern of life. It is still largely an individual struggle. But this process may, in the obscure future, turn into a collective effort crystallizing in an organized urban community life, and these African communities will almost inevitably have a Western and not an African character. But even before that stage is reached, the urban and the rural African may find that they have become complete strangers to each other.

9

THE CHANGING RÔLES
OF AFRICAN WOMEN

(Southern Rhodesia)

by J. F. Holleman

In the tribal areas of Southern Rhodesia the casual visitor is struck by the constant industry of women in their dusty kraals and often delapidated thatched huts, their toiling in the fields, or fetching water in pots and gourds often from a considerable distance away. It seems a pretty hard life for the rural housewife, with little time for relaxation and recreation, especially when compared with the life of their menfolk. No wonder that those whose knowledge of tribal society is derived from casual acquaintance with it, believe that women in traditional society are chattels and their existence a form of slavery. When one then observes in the new neatly laid-out urban settlements that all or most of the outward signs of domestic drudgery and hardship are absent, it is only natural to expect that a greater freedom, happiness and dignity has come in the life of the African women in the town.

Perhaps it is the bright appearance of the new African townships, the thousands of neatly-spaced cottages, which gives rise to this expectation. It is true that we still have a few urban slums, but both government and municipalities in Southern Rhodesia are making tremendous efforts to provide adequate and attractive accommodation for the steady stream of Africans to the urban areas. In a small city like Bulawayo, for instance, since

1954, two new townships for a total of nearly 6,000 tenar
families have arisen, one of these under a large governmen
sponsored scheme. And in this scheme, next door to the town
industries, Africans will be the owners of the properties the
occupy.

You have to be on the spot to realize what this means to
fledgling country in which, not so many years ago, the urba
African was only a bird of passage, paying a short visit to tow
in order to earn some cash. The new townships have helped t
change that, and the home-ownership schemes make th
change irrevocable because they give the urban African a sense
stability and security such as only ownership of a house ar
piece of ground can give.

In this new environment the women go about their hous
hold chores in a leisurely manner, cook the family meal ov
the little wood-stoves that are provided for them, tap wat
from standpipes, and tend their vegetables and flower beds
the little gardens while keeping an eye on their children playin
about in the sunshine.

The contrast with the rural domestic scene is there, f
anyone to see. It is therefore often a shock to find that, in sp
of the improved domestic facilities, the nicely furnished in
teriors and the opportunities for leisure and recreation, the urba
housewife herself does not generally think that her position ar
status have much improved. Indeed, it is especially the bette
educated, better-to-do minority, the wives of teachers, ministe
of religion and clerks, who voice the complaint that, in genera
the position and status of the housewife in urban society
probably worse than it is in the tribal communities.

What then is their main difficulty? Surprisingly enough the
do not immediately blame the shortage of money and hig
cost of living, or the government or city council, or Eur
peans generally, which the African male has chosen as l

vourite scapegoats. With quiet outspokenness they blame in
e first place their menfolk and husbands for 'holding them
wn' and preventing them from playing their full and
gitimate part in this new life. And here, perhaps in an over-
mplified manner, they have indicated the crux of what may
ell be the toughest problem which urban African society has
solve.

To explain this I must first return to the traditional social
ttern, in which the life of an individual, man, woman or
ild, is wrapped up in an intricately woven, carefully balanced
d very widespread fabric of kinship relation. In this 'web of
nship', as Professor Fortes calls it, a person's social position
more or less nicely balanced between relatives (by blood or
marriage) who are superior, and those who are subordinate.
his is not merely a matter of formality, of taking care to use the
rrect form of address. It involves a code of behaviour and a
ttern of social order in which every person meeting another
rson within this web of kinship, is either expected to extend
rvice, obedience or courtesy to the other, or is entitled to
ceive it. Depending on the particular type or nearness of the
lationship, these social obligations are discharged with vary-
g degrees of strictness or with varying measures of familiarity.
he point to remember is that these relationships are so wide-
read that they involve most of the people with whom a
rson regularly comes into contact in the neighbourhood.

Now, when we, as Europeans, think of the position of
omen in any society, we are inclined to see them mainly as
ives of husbands or as mothers of children, thereby over-
oking all the other relationships in which they may find
emselves. Moreover, in the types of tribal society which
ists in Southern Rhodesia, the position of a woman as a wife
d mother is *weaker* than in any other kind of relationship
though any anthropologist will probably tell you that even

this position is not nearly as weak as a paper analysis woul[
allow). But it is when we turn to the other relationships in
woman's life that we find her social and even legal stat[
growing to a remarkable extent, more indeed than we ev[
credited to our own womenfolk before they won the battle [
their emancipation.

The age-old institution of marrying a wife upon the promi[
or delivery of a sizeable bridewealth to her family is, in spite [
all anthropological writing, still widely regarded by Europea[
as a form of 'buying a wife'. Yet this institution gives her [
effective a security against marital abuse as could be devised, f[
a cruel husband not only runs the risk of losing his wife but [
also impairs his claim for the return of the bridewealth he h[
given for her. Moreover, it places a woman in a strong positi[
in regard to her brother and brother's wife. In Mashonalan[
for instance, a normal bridewealth is so high that few fathe[
could afford one for their sons were it not for the fact that t[
daughters of the family, by marrying into other famili[
provide the necessary marriage cattle for their brothers' wiv[
The kinship system takes full account of this by making t[
woman *vamwene* ('keeper') of her brother's wife. She is t[
obvious arbitrator in her brother's marital disputes; she is [
law the executrix of his estate when he dies, and she is t[
respected confidante and *vatete* ('female father') of his childre[

It is, however, as the mother of married daughters that [
woman attains her strongest position; that is, as a mother-i[
law to her sons-in-law and their families. In this relationsh[
her position does not rest only on considerations of a soci[
and legal character. Among the Mashona and kindred tribes [
receives powerful support from the deeply rooted mystic[
concepts of fertility and procreation. As the mother of a you[
wife she is seen as the immediate link with the matrilin[
ancestresses from which the power of procreation is derive[

er favour or disfavour towards her daughter's family-in-law
ay spell the difference between a fruitful and a childless
arriage. It is obvious then that this family will treat her with
e utmost respect and even servility.

Nor are these relationships expressed merely in the services
d courtesies which are extended to her. Prescribed by law,
d further enforced by the fear of mystical retribution, a
mber of material benefits are due to her. The most important
these is the 'motherhood beast', a cow or heifer payable by
r son-in-law upon or after her daughter's marriage. The
otherhood beast can be retained by the woman, a significant
fference from the actual bridewealth, which is a floating
set of the bride's *paternal* family, or from some other gifts of
all livestock which are earmarked for immediate ritual
crifice. The motherhood beast forms the beginning of a
metimes very considerable maternal estate, which falls out-
de the control of the woman's husband or her paternal
latives.

These few examples illustrate that in tribal society there are
lationships in a woman's life which, in a very real sense,
mpensate the comparative weakness in which she finds her-
lf as a wife and mother in the domestic environment of her
isband's family.

All this still applies at the present day in most of the rural
mmunities in Southern Rhodesia. For even school education
d a spreading Christianity have made no serious inroads
on it. Wherever the traditional fabric of tribal society has
mained more-or-less intact, a woman will find not only the
ildren of her own brothers and the husbands of her own
ughters who pay homage to her, but a multitude of others
ho, on the strength of this classificatory kinship system, are
aced in similar relations to her and therefore obliged to treat
r in a similar respectful manner.

As long as the web of kinship is intact. And here lies the gre
and inevitable difficulty of the women in the new urban cor
munities. For, in this heterogeneous town population, flocke
together from half-a-dozen different countries and scores
different tribal backgrounds, a woman may find a few sca
tered relatives, but no kinship system. There are the loose ar
often frayed bits of tribal culture from many origins, a fe
traditional concepts commonly shared. But these do not near
add up to a recognized code of behaviour or etiquette, let alor
a cohesive pattern of social order.

A large proportion of the urban population consists of sing
men, who are still birds of passage and no respecters of respec
able women. The rest is made up of a multiplicity of sma
family units, in which a woman is first and last the wife of
husband and the mother of his children. In other words, in tl
as yet unformed urban society the otherwise balanced patte
of a woman's social relationships is virtually monopolized l
the one kinship relationship in which she is traditional
weakest. Moreover, on this husband-and-wife relationship tl
hand of tradition weighs perhaps even more heavily in tov
than in tribal society. First, because most town people st
maintain individual contact with their rural background, ar
this impedes the acceptance and growth of a new soc
concept in which man and wife are equal partners. Secondl
because the short history of African town life has also seen tl
emergence of a new and daring class of easy-going women wl
take advantage of the ill-balance between the sexes by leadir
a relatively comfortable life as prostitutes; or, slightly mo
honourably, as short-term companions of men whose wives a
at their rural homes. With masculine inconsistency many m
secretly admire these glamour girls (the so-called 'spares'
delightful term !), but they dislike even taking their own wiv
and daughters out in public, to dances or cinemas. For there

e fear that their reputation might be associated with that of
e light-hearted creatures who frequent these places.

And so, in spite of more time for leisure and the cultural and
creational facilities around her, the faithful wife of a self-
specting husband is even more strictly tied to her neat
ottage in the township than she ever was to her rural home-
ead. This makes it difficult for her to widen the circle of
iends which she might make among the strangers in her
eighbourhood. In fact, what the student of rural African
ociety regretfully misses in the townships is the congenial
pect of fairly large and happy parties of neighbouring house-
ives gathered for a common social or economic pursuit.
here is no denying the loneliness, confused disillusion and
metimes bitterness of hundreds of women who are aware of
e possibility of a full and rich urban community life, but
em unable to attain it.

This, then, appears on the reverse side of the promising
cture presented by the neatly planned townships spread out
ader the bright African sky. It is, I think, an inevitable part of
e labour pains which must be suffered with the birth of this
ew society.

What can we, as administrators, do about it? Very little, I
n afraid. It is not the sort of problem that is solved by legis-
tion or by-laws; nor by the domestic guidance offered by helpful
elfare workers and European ladies' societies, however useful
ese efforts may be from other points of view. What we can
o, and what we are doing, is to unlock the doors which might
ar a woman from entering public life. But it would be foolish
force her out into the open. What we can do, and are doing
n an increasing scale, is to give her advice and guidance on
ow to run her household, how to look after her children, how
make her home attractive with simple and inexpensive
eans. We do this to give her confidence in an environment

which must often be strange and confusing to her. Al
because we hope that it will give her husband a new pride
his home, wife and family. And we try to encourage the kii
of cultural activity in which both men and women, ai
preferably married couples, participate. For we think that tl
will foster a sense of equality and mutual respect between tl
sexes. Useful efforts, which, here and there, may bear a litt
fruit. But they cannot solve the problem, for the real chan;
must come from within.

Perhaps it has started already: the wife of an African M.
sharing her husband's public duties; a minister's wido
staunchly taking care of her late husband's parish; a circle
young housewives meeting to discuss the problems of the
urban community; a hesitant effort by factory girls to for
their own workers' union; a cultural society encouragi
women to become members; the married couples singing si
by side in a newly formed choral society. Isolated instances, .
of these. But they may be the early symptoms of a growii
awareness that with the loss of a widely active kinship syste
the relationship between husband and wife must make roo
for a new concept of marital and social partnership. With
this single frame they must now seek to balance the relati
weakness and strength which formerly derived from multip
kinship relations extending far beyond domestic life. This
the type of marriage relationship counselled by the Christi
Church, but as the Church has found, it does not come l
simple bidding.

IO

THE STATUS OF AFRICAN WOMEN

by H. J. Simons

The change taking place in the status of African women is one of the important things affecting South Africa. It is misleading to say that the women are 'emerging' from a state of servitude, or even of submissiveness, for in their traditional society they were not secluded in any kind of oriental *purdah* or trained to be docile and subdued. Indeed, they hold important positions in some tribes, such as the Swazi, where power is shared by the king and his mother, or the Transvaal Lovedu, who are governed by a line of queens, the *Mujajis*, widely famed as rainmakers, and the inspiration of Rider Haggard's story of 'She-who-must-be-obeyed'. Even ordinary women had the right under tribal law to sue or be sued, control arable land, and possess property acquired by work and as gifts. Venda women use such property to give as bridewealth for women who become their so-called 'wives', performing for them some of the same duties as women who are married to men – a practice that European courts have declared to be immoral and contrary to public policy.

Nevertheless the family in South African tribes – as distinct from matrilineal peoples like the Bemba farther north – was polygynous, patriarchal and patrilineal, that is to say, male-dominated. Girls left their village at marriage to join the husband; and a man might establish his own homestead after marrying and having children, but the patriarchal group was much more self-contained, closely knit and stable than the

family in European or present-day African society. Function
were divided between men and women, each sex exercisin
leadership in its own sphere, and where these clashed it was th
man who formally and legally, if not actually, took decisio
and acted on behalf of all. Public affairs, the business of settlin
law cases, the big tribal gatherings to discuss policy, and th
making of war were also reserved to the men.

Now in the modern and increasingly Westernized societ
African women are beginning to claim and fulfil many of th
rôles and functions previously held by men, and to think (
themselves as individuals and not only in terms of the
relations to families and kinship groups in which men play th
leading part. This process is, however, considerably held up b
certain conflicts between these facts of social change and th
legal systems which operate in the Union and regulate th
status of women.

It is these difficulties which I am going to consider; and th
first thing to say is that, for Africans, three different leg;
systems are operative, and these systems do not speak with on
voice. They frequently command different courses, or expre
different moral values, and many an individual is caught up i
bewilderment and personal disaster.

The first system is the customary law of the tribe to whic
every African is presumed to belong, though many thousan
of men and women today actually have no tribal affiliation
Tribal systems are varied, and I shall avoid going into deta
about them. It will, perhaps, be obvious that many of th
customary rules affecting women are not suitable today, (
desired by women who are breaking away from tribalisr
whether they have left the rural areas or not. Such women a
discovering through education, Christianity and hard e:
perience as breadwinners that they suffer disabilities as wom(
under their own tribal laws.

The second system, known here as Native law, is based upon European interpretations and amendments to tribal laws. It is applied, exclusively to Africans, by the Native courts, which are presided over by European administrators. Legislatures and courts have set themselves the aim of freeing the tribal law of what in European eyes are blemishes: the punishment of sorcerers, marriages arranged by family heads for their children, or the transfer of children from one family to another in settlement of marriage debts. Both bride and bridegroom must now consent to marriage; widows cannot be forced to bear children in the name of their deceased husband. These are changes inspired by the reformer anxious to rescue women from subjugation, but there are other modifications that bear the imprint of a juristic concept drawn from the individualistic society of the West and imposed on the very different kinship and economic pattern of the tribe. It is something of a paradox that under this Westernized version of tribal law, women's rights have been whittled down in important respects.

The third system is European law, the common law of the land, which in South Africa is Roman-Dutch law. For the individual African this often acts as a kind of safety-valve; its application to Africans dates from a more liberal past, when policy was framed with a view to assimilating Africans and Europeans into a common economic, legal and political system. It is one of South Africa's anomalies that whereas all African women are denied the vote, they have the right to avail themselves of the common law, by which they may, without restraint, achieve the status of European women in matters of marriage, guardianship, contracts and proprietory capacity.

The conflict between this Roman-Dutch law and Native law will be apparent when it is realized that generally speaking, and

ignoring local variations, under Native law women are treate
as perpetual minors. They may not own, inherit or bequea
property. They may not enter into contracts. They may n
enter into a Native law marriage without the consent of the
father, brother or other male guardian. They cannot exerci
rights of guardianship over their children even if unmarrie
widowed or divorced.

In Natal where these limitations under Native law a
enforced most strictly, an unmarried, widowed or divorce
woman may be freed from the control of her father or guardia
by Court order if she satisfies the judicial officer that she is fit t
be freed, but this is not easily done. In an actual case where
father refused to grant his daughter permission to become
nun, the Court decided not to overrule his objections.

There are numerous instances where widows placed
Native law under the guardianship of their deceased husband
brother are denied access to the deceased's estate and are virtuall
compelled to watch its dissipation by the heir without practic
remedy. Another common source of hardship arises from th
tribal system of land tenure in the Reserves, which exclud
widows and daughters from the inheritance of real estate, an
allows them only the right of permissive use as long as the
remain unmarried.

Now it may be claimed that in respect of the guardianshi
over women, Native law does not differ substantially from mo
systems of tribal law. It is true that in the traditional society th
widow in most South African tribes would be taken care of b
one of her late husband's brothers, if she had no son, or if h
son was a minor. The brother would have to provide her wit
land and help her as though she were his wife. Indeed, under
custom known as *ukungena* meaning 'to enter', he or son
other relative of the deceased was expected to have childr
by the widow, these being regarded sociologically and legal

the legitimate offspring of the dead man. The tribal attitude as that a widow's reproductive capacity or sexual needs ould not be neglected because of her husband's untimely ath. This attitude and emphasis is different from that which gards the woman as a perpetual minor. The results might ten be the same, were it not, again, for the fact that the ibal way of life even in rural areas has changed considerably, d in important ways.

Nowadays, for example, *ukungena* tends to fall into disrepute, rtly because missionaries and their converts think it is imoral, and partly because of the shortage of land. Heirs are ger to take possession of the plot occupied by the widow and r daughters and often neglect and harass them so as to drive em off the land and take occupation themselves.

If the widow is a Christian and was married by Christian tes she cannot enter into a *ukungena* relationship. Her prospects remarriage are comparatively small. Consequently a great mber of widows are found in both rural and urban areas ithout male guardianship even where Native law continues to at them as minors.

In the old social order, now rapidly disintegrating, neither en nor women lived independently of a family group. There ere few unmarried women or men. A woman had security, d an assured social position within the family, whether as ughter, wife or mother. Property was not for the most part dividually owned, but was attached to the domestic group der the care of the head who administered it in the interests of members, women as well as men.

This collective and co-operative kinship group has been eatly disorganized under the pressure of Western individual onomics, education and religion. Not more than 10% of frican husbands have more than one wife today, for polygyny s become a luxury. With the decline of polygyny has gone

the large extended family of the old society. We are witnessin
the emergence of the simple monogamous family group tha
seems to be the universal type of domestic unit in our presen
industrialized and urbanized civilization.

Other changes are the growth of individual ownership, an
reluctance to accept kinship obligations. Large numbers c
young men and women leave home to earn an independen
living as domestic servants, factory workers, nurses, teacher
and traders. Contrary to the old standard, there are man
unmarried, widowed, divorced or deserted women who, i
fact, exercise power of guardianship and act as heads of house
holds in both town and country.

Many individuals in a state of transition from tribal cultur
to a new type of society observe customs drawn from bot
sources. Africans combine the *lobola* institution (the practice c
handing over cattle or other valuable consideration to th
bride's father) with a Christian or civil rites marriage. It is nc
uncommon for men to be married at one time to differer
women under European and Native law, although the Nativ
law marriage in such circumstances is not valid.

The co-existence of two types of marriage in one societ
gives rise to conflicts and anomalies. Take the instance of
polygynist with four or five wives who is converted t
Christianity. The missionary tells him to put aside all his wive
except one whom he must marry in the Church. He then ha
the problem of disposing of the other, now ex-wives. Nativ
law, or tribal law as interpreted by the Courts to suit this nev
situation (which obviously could not have arisen in the ol
society) says that the husband has a duty to maintain and care fc
the ex-wives as long as they remain in his village or homestea
under his tutelage, but he may not, of course, co-habit wit
them.

This case illustrates the kind of legal relationship that exis tween the Christian marriage and the Native law marriage, as it is known here, the customary union. In deference to e Church's views the Christian marriage has been given a gher status. An African who is a partner to a customary union ay, without divorcing his wife, enter into a Christian or civil arriage with another woman whereupon the customary ion is automatically dissolved. On the other hand, if a man s married in church he cannot during the subsistence of this arriage enter into a customary union, for this would be garded as immoral, entitling his wife to divorce on the ounds of adultery.

Yet unlawful polygyny of this kind is not uncommon. It ay occur when the wife of a Christian marriage is childless, or the marriage is otherwise unsuccessful, and the husband, thout getting a divorce, hands over cattle for another oman. In law this union is illicit, however, and children born it are illegitimate.

These occurrences are not to be construed as a 'reversion to e primitive'. The 'mixed culture' situation is the result of a nflict between two dissimilar ways of life and an imperfect justment to conflicting values. The process of adaptation is t made easier by the political and economic restrictions of e colour bar and racial segregation.

Segregation perpetuates the migrant labour system, which eatly affects marriage and family life. Half a million adult en, two-thirds of them between 18 and 40 years, are at any e time temporarily absent from their homes in the reserves. e number of women temporarily absent is very much less. e urban population, in consequence, has a surplus of ,000 males, and the reserves a surplus of 600,000 females. e disproportions are being accentuated by the Administra- n's policy of expelling family groups and individual women m urban areas. By March 1957, 2,868 families and 2,881

women without families had been removed from the Cap
Peninsula and adjoining regions. The unbalanced sex rati
together with the instability of migrant communities and th
insecurity of African life in urban areas, is playing havoc wi
the family organization. Reliable figures are lacking, but it
certain that a large proportion of couples in the larger tow
are not married by either Native or European law, and th
there is a widespread practice in some reserves of dispensi
with all formalities at marriage and resorting to the *ukuthwala*
form of elopement or abduction.

It is evident that the tribal law, meaning here both customa
and Native law, no longer corresponds to reality. Whatever
says, women are not subject to perpetual guardianship. The
work, earn wages and acquire property, and in the course of
doing enter into contracts. They do marry without the conse
of their parents; or, failing that, enter into extra-marital unio
They do exercise guardianship over their children.

For the Westernized African woman who has outgro
tribal law, there remains the right of appeal to the common la
of the land, the Roman-Dutch law, which very often is the
salvation as individuals. But there is no doubt that mo
African women do not know that they possess this righ
Many who do know are deterred from using it by their me
folk, who, like men everywhere, are reluctant to admit wom
to the privileges which are exclusively their own. Many m
object, for instance, to land being inherited by widows an
daughters on the ground that, if they marry, the estate will pa
from the family to the hands of an alien kinship group.

The attitude of the Administration is somewhat ambiguou
On the one hand it is committed to encouraging the spread
Christianity, and in so far as it provides a modern education,
transmits corresponding ideas of individual freedom and se
equality. On the other hand it is State policy to preser

ibalism, and this entails maintaining male domination so that
nancipation of women is not encouraged.

Women, however, have a trump card to play which they are
ound to use with increasing effect. This is their growing
fluence in the national organizations. Here their services are
alued by their menfolk, and the more important they become
. the movement for the removal of the colour bar and segrega-
on laws, the more they will press their claims to the removal
˙ the disabilities they suffer as women. We must, therefore,
nticipate the growth of a feminist movement within the
amework of African nationalism. The pressure for feminine
nancipation is bound to stimulate and accelerate the pressure
·r political emancipation. Both aims are included in the
·ogramme of the South African Women's Federation, which
presents women of all races. It organized the great procession
f 20,000 women that handed over the petition against passes to
ie Prime Minister at the Union Buildings, Pretoria, on
h August 1956.

But this very fact, whereby the women's political activities
·come a strong weapon against the conservatism of African
.en, also, on the other hand, leads them into increased political
ld legal difficulties with the Administration. An African
·oman was recently convicted for living in Cape Town
ithout a permit and deported under police escort to her home
˙ the Transkei. She left her three children with her husband,
• whom she had been married for 16 years. The Crown
leged that she had not lived in Cape Town for the full 15 years
quired by law to establish a legal defence against eviction
om an urban area.

It was on this technical ground that she was convicted and
·ported. She and her associates, however, are convinced that
tion was taken against her because she played a leading rôle in
·e local branch of the women's organization attached to the

African National Congress, the chief political organization of Africans in the Union. The Appellate Division has upheld her appeal against the conviction, but she is now one of the 15 accused in the treason trial in Johannesburg. [July 1957.]

Here, as in Europe, the decisive factor is likely to be the rôle of women in public affairs and as wage-earners. Early attempts to emancipate them by legal reforms failed because they were premature and lacked the appropriate social basis. With the decline of liberalism, a policy of 'legal segregation' was practised which, combined with a narrow and rigid formalism led the courts to depress women's status in many respects below that of the old tribal law. Now it is the Native law that lags behind social practice. There is as yet no concerted movement to make the law conform to usage, partly because the disenfranchized African population has no power to decide such matters, and partly because the men, being in the more favourable position, are not inclined to sponsor such a movement. But the discordance between law and practice is only one ingredient in a complex situation resulting from a great social upheaval, which is uniting a multiplicity of small, intimate social groups into an urbanized, mechanized multi-racial state. I do not doubt that tribal culture – magic, ancestor worship, polygyny, clans, a subsistence economy, chieftainship – all these will be dissipated and erased in the process, and that African men and women will embrace the ideals of human dignity and equality that have always inspired the emancipator.

I I

SLUMS AND HOUSING SCHEMES

by F. M. L. Stoker

ᴉe of the greatest problems that have arisen in Africa is that
providing housing for the tens of thousands of all races who
ᴇ flocking to the towns in search of work. England partially
ᴠed the problem in the eighteenth century by the system of
ᴇd cottages' which had worked well in rural areas. This
ᴁtem is used in the Union by the mines and by one or two
ᴦe industrial undertakings on the Rand, but is practically
ᴦn-existent in other South African towns, where indescribably
ᴅdid slum conditions have grown up, just outside the civic
ᴁndaries.

ᴉn South Africa two factors tend to encourage this type of
ᴁm dwelling: moderately rapid though expensive transport,
ᴅd climatic conditions which make not weatherproof or
ᴄmfortable but *possible* dwellings out of corrugated iron
ᴁter tanks cut in half, or mud hovels with roofs of over-
ᴘping bits of old tin or corrugated iron and wooden boxes,
ᴛh the worst leaks plugged with scraps of rag or sacking. The
ᴁter supply may, in such areas, come from stand-pipes as far
ᴧ a quarter of a mile apart. The drainage system is non-
ᴀstent. The thrice-weekly night-soil removal is totally
ᴅdequate when three times the statutory number of people
ᴇ the conveniences. Add to all this ten to twelve hours of
ᴀ-tropical sunshine daily, intermittent thunderstorms, and a
ᴇdley of Europeans, Coloureds, Chinese, Indians and Africans

89

sharing the amenities with fowls, ducks, geese, donkeys, goa
and cattle, and you get, for example, a fair picture of Korste
outside Port Elizabeth, in 1936, when Sir E. Thornton describe
it as 'the worst slum in the world'.

There are many such slums now, but some of the difficulti
involved in the problem of slum clearance, wherever it
undertaken, and more particularly when this happens und
African conditions, can clearly be illustrated from a study
the Coloured population from Korsten and other parts of th
city, who were rehoused in the Schauder Township Sub
economic Housing Scheme. The passage of years since th
scheme began has made it possible to study and form conclu
sions about the real or long-term effects of rehousing, which th
initial immediate relief from slum dwellings often obscures.

Medical Officers of Health had repeatedly warned Po
Elizabeth of the dangers of bubonic plague, and in 1938 pla
were nearing completion for extensive sub-economic housin
to replace the Korsten slum, when the first case of plagu
occurred. The outbreak cost the city of Port Elizabeth, direct
and indirectly, nearly £34,000, and revolutionized the counci
attitude to the provision of housing for its growing mult
racial population.

It would take too long to enumerate the various econom
and legal difficulties involved in servicing and rebuilding such
congested slum area as Korsten. The council decided, in view
all the factors involved, that its economic and sub-econom
housing schemes should be erected on new land. This mea
providing all the essential services, but the outlay could I
included in the capital cost, met by government loan at $\frac{3}{4}$
interest (for sub-economic housing) and redeemable in 4
years. An excellent scheme, had provision been made f
outside supervision of the calculation of rents; for rents
subsidized housing can be considered from two viewpoin

irst, the purely economic, that of the city treasurer, which
ncludes provision for defaulting tenants, repairs, insurance,
nterest and redemption, renewals, street lighting, street clean-
ng, and the maintenance of the normal essential services,
nereby constituting a valuable asset to the city and not a
ability. And the second or social viewpoint, which brings to
ght important consideration of the amount of rent a rehoused
um family can afford to pay, in addition to providing adequate
utrition for its members. It is here that opinion is sharply
ivided. Let it be said at once, that the rents charged are by no
neans excessive for the type of accommodation, and that they
ompare very favourably with those paid for comparable
nunicipal houses in England at the time they were completed.
Nevertheless it is on the solution of this problem of providing
dequate nutrition, when rent and the cost of transport to work
f the breadwinner have been met, that the whole social value
f sub-economic housing really hinges. The difficulty is
omplicated by the high cost of transport to work from these
eripheral areas. The problem is not solved even in economic
rms by using a bicycle or walking, for such an expenditure of
nergy requires extra nourishment if health is to be maintained.

It is clear, therefore, that if sub-economic housing is really
 be effective, rents must be assessed with reference to the basic
utritional needs of each tenant family. This can be achieved only
y a planned system of differential renting, which involves highly
pecialized administrative techniques; and in the war years,
hen the bulk of these houses were built, this was impossible.

A few figures are necessary to give an idea of the scale of this
heme, and they are greatly to the credit of Port Elizabeth.
etween 1938 and 1942, 160 three-bedroomed sub-economic
ouses were built for Europeans at a rent of 12s. 3d. per week,
d a further 142 two-bedroomed houses reconditioned at
. 6d. per week. For Coloureds, 100 three-bedroomed

houses at 11s. 4d. per week were built and 1,400 two-be
roomed houses, at rentals varying from 6s. 6d. to 9s. 4d. p
week; and for Africans, several thousand houses at low
rentals were constructed at New Brighton. It is not witho
interest that in this way, several years before the Group Are
Act, Port Elizabeth, along with other municipalities, w
gradually rehousing slum populations in homogeneous rac
areas, without friction or adverse comment.

What about the social point of view? The change fro
living in a single-roomed mud hovel, to a three- or fo
roomed house, had many unexpected results. Even in Englar
where the contrast between slum conditions and municip
housing was not nearly so great, it was several years befo
public health authorities realized that the removal of slu
populations to hygienic houses might, against all expectatio
result in increased morbidity and higher death rates. O
reason for this is that in South Africa, as elsewhere, there
considerable evidence that sub-letting of rooms by slu
tenants is a recognized source of income during times
financial difficulty. It often results in gross overcrowding, bu
does tend to increase the amount of money available for foc
This practice is usually prohibited by the leases of the ne
housing schemes into which the slum dwellers are move
This was the case in Schauder Township in which the Colour
population of Korsten was rehoused, but owing to acu
shortage of accommodation it has since been allowed.

Then again, in slums, social pressures to obtain dece
furniture are absent, but in most sub-economic housin
tenants feel they must supplement their inadequate possessio
and in Africa, certainly in Schauder Township, this led to
outlay out of all proportion to income. Furthermore, u
scrupulous agents were constantly at work offering iniquito
hire-purchase agreements to gullible uneducated folk. T

Hire Purchase Act of 1942 as amended, has done much to remedy the position, but in the early years heavy monthly payments tended to curtail still further the amount of money available for food.

Then again, the accepted standard of cleanliness is much higher in sub-economic housing; as one woman put it, 'Cleanliness may be next to godliness, but it costs a lot more!' The social stigma of having to put badly patched and darned clothes out on the line to dry, is an added incentive to buy new ones, again at the expense of food. Electric light, even with the shilling-in-the-slot meters, costs more than candles. The shopping centres being two-and-a-half to four miles away necessitates at least one additional return bus fare per week.

The provision of hygienic up-to-date government schools, and the considerable social pressure (now enforced by statute in urban areas) to send children to school at an earlier age and to keep them there to a later age, increases the amount spent on education, both directly and indirectly. Although education in these schools is free, the cost of school books and the necessity for supplying reasonably decent clothing makes heavy demands on the family purse. In short, it is clear that it costs a family more to live in a decent house than it does to live in a slum, quite apart from paying higher rent and transport costs.

The problem facing any housing authority is therefore the provision of adequate living conditions for a population with such a low earning capacity, that, during the years when the children are small and requiring nourishing food, the amount that can with safety be afforded for rent is ridiculously low. The Port Elizabeth City Council started out with the idea that the enjoyment of good housing would spur the families to greater efforts, in order to remain in them. It was not realized that in most cases economy on food was the only way in which the tenants could hope to meet the increased rent.

The financial squeeze showed itself in two clearly define
ways: the emergence of pulmonary tuberculosis in families no
known to have had infected members on rehousing; and i
the large number of families who moved from houses at high
rents to less expensive ones, or left the township altogethe
owing anything from ten shillings to thirty-five pounds te
shillings in rent. Analysis of the destination of tenant famili
leaving Schauder Township revealed that of the 847 tenan
who left the estate, 93.9% had definitely not been rehabilitate
Further, of the 663 tenant families known to be directl
infected with pulmonary tuberculosis, 30% had left sub
economic housing, and in the majority of cases had returned t
slum conditions.

As yet, no adequate methods of measuring the health of an
population in objective terms have been devised, but the crud
vital statistics for Schauder Township, compared with those f
the Coloured population of the rest of Port Elizabeth, give som
indication of the effects of sub-economic housing.

The crude death rate in Schauder Township (average 24.3
per thousand) was below that of the Coloured population in th
rest of the city in the years 1944 to 1946, but above it in th
following two years, though the average for the five years wa
very similar. The crude birth rate showed a markedly high
tendency in Schauder Township in each of the years und
review, averaging 6.33.

The infantile mortality rate, which is considered by some t
be the best index to the condition of the general environment,
smaller in Schauder Township, by as much as an average (
46.7 per thousand live births, for the five years 1944 to 194
inclusive. This would suggest, that the general environment i
Schauder Township is markedly superior to that of th
Coloured population in the remainder of the city, and do
indicate the overall environmental advantage of sub-econom

ousing. Probably the excellent clinic facilities available were partly responsible. Nevertheless, the average infantile mortality ate, over the five years, was three times as great as the average *European* rate for the same period. This fact is vital, in that ub-economic housing is supposed to provide the minimum physical standards for the maintenance of health.

I mentioned the incidence of tuberculosis as one of the most disturbing indices of the financial pressures involved in re-ousing. The average pulmonary tuberculotic death rate in chauder Township for these five years was 36.99 per thousand eaths as contrasted with only 24.26 for the rest of the Coloured population of Port Elizabeth. This is in striking contrast to the crude death rate, and suggests that pulmonary tuberculosis nay well be one of the most serious factors neutralizing the expected effects of a healthy environment. It must be remem-ered that a large number of persons are infected by tubercle, ut the disease remains dormant unless environmental condi-ions (such as strain and malnutrition) lower the body's esistance. The emergence of new cases in families which had esided for several years in sub-economic housing may, there-ore, be attributed to both direct and indirect factors. Direct actors, such as infection from workmates, neighbours, chools, public buildings, travelling in buses with active cases, ving in contaminated houses; indirect factors, such as the dded strain of a longer journey to work by bus, cycling or walking, those using the bus often having to wait for long eriods in all weathers at peak hours; malnutrition, because of ncreased overhead expenditure due to living in sub-economic ousing.

The very fact that the houses are so well built may give rise o a further possibility of infection. When the weather is cold nd blankets are few and thin, the temptation to seal up rooms o keep out the cold is almost irresistible. It is quite impossible to exclude all fresh air from a mud hovel, or a wood and irc shack, but with well-fitting windows and doors shut, in a wel built brick house, the result is quite different, more especially the dwelling is overcrowded at night.

Rehabilitation, in the generally accepted sense of the teri means to restore people to efficient functioning in the con munity; it does not merely mean rehousing; and there com a point where it is more to the family's advantage to remain slum dwellings and to refuse the type of rehabilitation offere This may seem a harsh conclusion, but it is reached after, and spite of, careful consideration of the disease and degradatic which the conditions of slum dwellings themselves engender.

Slums in South Africa are so appalling that many people a led to believe that relief from such physical conditions is itself the essential step. This survey has shown that it is not s and that for many families the very reverse is true, particular among non-Europeans, to whom our present-day industri revolution has brought such drastic social upheaval and ir balance. It would appear, therefore, that the choice before t city councils of the Union is, either to leave in their slu environment those slum dwellers who are unable to obtain income adequate for basic needs, or to make genuine r habilitation possible, by a system of differential renting based scientifically assessed capacity to pay. Such a scheme is the on permanent solution of the problem of abolishing slums, a rehousing *all* slum dwellers with even the minimum services necessary for health and decency.

I2

TRIBAL ELDERS TO TRADE UNIONS

by A. L. Epstein

The Copperbelt of Northern Rhodesia comprises a narrow strip of land which runs for about two hundred miles along the boundary of the Belgian Congo. Little more than a generation ago it was mostly an area of bush, which carried a small and scattered population of African tribesmen. Today its townships and locations carry a population of some 25,000 Europeans and nearly 250,000 Africans, all of them dependent in one way or another on the copper mining industry.

There is a sense in which the Copperbelt is one of the great 'social laboratories' of Africa: here one can study in relatively small compass the processes of social change at work over the whole continent. I have been particularly interested, in my own researches, in an aspect of it which has also attracted a great deal of administrative and political attention – in some quarters, even alarm. That is the development of trade unionism, particularly among the African mine employees.

There is more to this development than a simple matter of Africans learning European methods of organization and 'copying' them. It has involved a radical break with time-hallowed ideas of authority based on lineage, age, or the possession of certain esoteric knowledge. So the development and acceptance of a new form of leadership has only been gradually achieved; its emergence has to be traced in the protracted struggles for prestige and power which have been a

marked feature of the growth of the African Copperbel
communities.

The Africans who first came to the Copperbelt in search o
work were not only truly tribal, but were drawn from a hos
of different tribes, each with its own distinctive body o
customs and values. They had, of course, no knowledge o
experience of urban life: they were a people whose life wa
bound up in a set of social relations which centred round th
land, their kinsmen, village headmen and chiefs. At first the
came as migrant labourers. Often they stayed no more than si
months before returning to their villages. Even today there is
high degree of coming and going and changing of jobs; bu
the trend towards more stable settlement in the towns i
unmistakable.

From the outset, African mine employees have been house
by the mining companies in vast compounds which ar
administered by a European compound manager and his staf
In the past the compound manager was assisted by a body o
company police, upon whom he relied to maintain disciplin
among the compound-dwellers. The compound police als
provide some liaison between the African workers and th
management. But this arrangement was found to be not wholl
satisfactory, and at some mines a system of representatio
through tribal elders was also introduced. On the Roa
Antelope Mine at Luanshya, for example, tribal elders cam
into being as early as 1931.

The elders were elected at meetings of their fellow tribesmen
Tribal elders were themselves mine employees, and were draw
from all departments of the mine. Some of them were un
skilled labourers, some were boss boys or charge hands, an
there were a few who were employed as mine clerks; but wha
is significant is that in nearly every case the elder could clai
close relationship with the tribal chief. Indeed, once selected

the elder would take upon himself the name of his chief, and was normally called by that name: he would receive from time to time gifts of beer, brought as tribute by his people according to ancient custom.

These elders formed a kind of advisory body to the compound manager. They were entitled to call for a meeting with him whenever they wanted to discuss matters affecting the social or working conditions of the people. At the same time, through the elders, the compound manager was able to convey to the mine employees the latest pronouncement of management policy. Individual elders were also called upon as occasion demanded to advise on points of African custom. For example, in order to gain married quarters and rations the mine employee had to show that he was legally married. Since the only form of union legally recognized amongst Africans was the marriage according to Native law and custom, the elders were often called upon to assist in establishing the validity or invalidity of marriages contracted by their tribesmen.

The system of elders proved most valuable to the compound manager, but there is little doubt that it was also widely popular among the people. The work of the elders extended to nearly every aspect of African life on the mine. Those who had disputes brought them before the elders and had them settled in accordance with customary modes of procedure. Those who had domestic troubles of one kind or another would go to their elder so that – to translate the vernacular expression – he might 'teach them to live properly in the house'. When a stranger arrived on the mine, he was at once directed to the house of the elder of his tribe, who would feed and look after him until his relatives had been traced. Whenever news was received of the death of a chief in the rural areas, people looked to their elder to make arrangements for carrying out the traditional mourning ceremonies. But above all this, the tribal elders were the representatives of their people in bringing grievances to the notice of the mine authorities.

The institution of tribal elders rested, of course, upon the assumption that the social ties which linked Africans to one another in the towns remained those of the tribal system; its corollary was that forms of authority which had their origin in that system were equally applicable on the mines. At the time there was, no doubt, some justification for that view. When quarrels flared up and developed into brawls, the participants aligned themselves with their fellow tribesmen. The very choice as elders of men of royal or chiefly blood was itself important in this respect. Their prestige derived from tribal political values; their appointment as elders was a reaffirmation of these values. Nevertheless, there was some indication as early as 1935 that the basic assumptions underlying the introduction of tribal elders were becoming out of step with the new conditions.

In 1935 serious disturbances occurred on the Copperbelt, particularly at Luanshya, where a mob of Africans stormed the compound office on the mine. A number of Africans were killed, and many others injured. In the strike situation the workers rejected the authority of the elders, who had to seek refuge in the compound office. In 1940 there was another strike which was again accompanied by violence. At Nkana mine 17 Africans were killed, and 63 injured. The rôle of the elders at this time was well brought out in the events which occurred at Mufulira. Here again it was clear that the elders had lost the confidence of the people, and they were accused of being in league with the Europeans. On the advice of the District Commissioner the workers at Mufulira appointed their own strike committee of 17, and the members of this committee acted as strike leaders until the dispute was settled. The strike leaders exercised effective control throughout the strike; at

Mufulira there were no incidents, and the days passed quietly until the strike came to an end. Here were the first signs that a new form of authority was emerging, a new urban leadership.

After the strike, the tribal elders or tribal representatives, as they now came to be known, continued to enjoy the support of government and the mines. Government labour officers were charged with the task of 'educating the tribal representatives to become intelligently familiar with all matters relating to native labour', and to teach them 'to present cases for the adjustment of labour conditions in a reasonable manner'. But the new urban communities had begun to take root, and soon the position of the tribal representatives came to be increasingly challenged by men of a different stamp.

The gradual change in the pattern of urban leadership emerges most clearly in the urban advisory councils. These councils were set up by the government in about 1941. They were designed to bring the Administration into closer touch with the local African population. The councils met regularly under the chairmanship of the local District Commissioner, and were supposed to bring to the attention of government matters of concern to the townspeople. They discussed such matters as conditions at the hospital, the lack of adequate water facilities in the compounds, the practice of the colour bar in European-owned shops, and so on. In the beginning the members of the councils were elected by the tribal representatives acting as an electoral college; and the early councils were in fact dominated by the tribal representatives.

At about the same time, however, bodies known as African welfare societies began to flourish in the urban centres. The welfare societies drew their membership mainly from the small numbers of educated Africans in the towns. The leading members were invariably teachers, clerks, and hospital orderlies. Significantly, their meetings were conducted in English, whereas those of the urban advisory council were still conducted in the vernacular.

The welfare societies were in no sense 'official' bodies and therefore could make no claim to represent the local community. They were avowedly non-political in their aims, but in fact as they developed they rapidly acquired political functions. They made representations to the local authorities on various matters, and were often able to get conditions improved and complaints attended to. Members of the welfare societies spoke of co-operation with the advisory councils. But the tensions between them soon became open. To administrative officers it looked as though the advisory councils were coming to take second place to the welfare societies. Eventually, the societies were granted direct representation on the advisory councils.

In the years which followed, the political influence of the tribal representatives rapidly declined. The mining companies were persuaded to give recognition to committees representing the interests of boss boys, and clerks' associations also began to make their appearance. By 1949, when the urban advisory councils were dissolved and new elections held, the tribal representatives had been largely replaced by leading figures in the welfare societies and clerks' associations.

The challenge to the position of the tribal representatives may be viewed from a number of aspects. In one way it may be seen as an expression of the opposition of different generations; in another of the clash between literate and illiterate. The Africans who were led to join the welfare societies were mostly younger men, and were certainly better educated than the tribal representatives. They were also more articulate on the specific problems of town life, in particular on their position as Africans within the new multi-racial communities. But these oppositions were themselves only a reflection of a wider con-

ct of values. The system of tribal elders was rooted in the
ommon view that the Copperbelt was only a place of tem-
orary sojourn: after a year or two African workers would
turn to their villages to resume the more even tenor of tribal
e. For the migrant labourer the tribal elder served as a
minder that although his home lay many hundreds of miles
vay, his deepest ties were still with kinsfolk in distant villages
d in allegiance to his chief, and that these ties were cemented
y a body of customs which divided him sharply from the
ople of other tribes amongst whom he lived and worked in
e towns. By contrast, the new leaders made their bid for
pport by appealing to the African as wage-earner and urban-
veller. Like the elders, the new leaders were also of rural
igin, but unlike the elders, they had committed themselves
the new industrial and multi-racial society that had grown
around the towns. In their professions as school-teachers,
hristian ministers and clerks they were themselves actively
gaged in pushing forward into a new form of society – a
ciety where clan affiliation, or attachment to village headman
d chief, were no longer of primary significance in ordering
cial relations. By virtue of their education, and proficiency in
iglish, these men became the intermediaries between the mass
all the African people and the European authorities: in their
nscious approximation to European standards in manner and
ess they were also providing a bridge between the two
ltures.

Thus it was that when trade unionism was first introduced to
fricans in Northern Rhodesia, the leadership in the new
ions was predominantly recruited from the class of clerks
d other more educated Africans – the very people who had
en leading members of the welfare societies. Hence, too,
any of the early union leaders came from Barotseland or
yasaland, whose peoples had a much longer educational

tradition, from missions and mission schools, than most of th
fellow Africans in the tribal areas of Northern Rhodesia.

The African Mine Workers Trade Union was established
1949. From the very beginning there were reports of fricti
between the Union executive and the tribal representati
about the division of their respective spheres of jurisdicti
These squabbles continued until the Union decided to press
the abolition of the tribal representatives. At length
Chamber of Mines agreed to consult the African mine employ
in the matter. About 80% of the 35,000 Africans employed
all mines on the Copperbelt voted against the retention
tribal representation. This was in 1953 – some three and a h
years after the formation of the Union. Later in the year
first popular elections by secret ballot were held for the urb
advisory councils. When the new councils reassembled tl
were almost entirely composed of the new leaders in the tra
union movement and the African National Congress.

The gradual disappearance of the tribal elders as a force
urban political life may be taken as an index of the degree
which Africans have become increasingly involved in the wa
earning economy and way of life of the towns. The ma
problems which now confront the urban African are mostl
though not entirely – of the kind which arise in any indust
community: for assistance in their solution he turns to the n
leaders in the trade unions and the National Congress.

It would I think be a gross over-simplification to conclu
that the passing of tribal representation on the Copperbelt a
marked the demise of urban tribalism itself. For example, i
interesting to notice that recent cleavages which have develo
within the African Mine Workers Union and the Afri
National Congress have been interpreted by Africans the
selves as expressions of tribal antagonisms. We touch here up
a very complex problem. The growth of the new url

mmunities has been marked at every stage by increasing
nomic and social differentiation, so that the new leadership
up is not itself homogeneous. I myself consider therefore
t these cleavages cannot be explained simply in terms of the
sistence of traditional tribal values; but it remains significant
t Africans themselves explain them in this way.

mention this at the end in case it is thought that the process
ave been describing, of the movement away from tribalism
the sphere of political representation, is either finally accom-
shed or extends over the entire field of social relations. That
uld be a misleading interpretation. The term 'tribalism' has
umber of quite distinct points of reference which are
netimes apt to be confused. Its closer definition, and the
ree to which it operates within the various sets of urban
ial relations are among the major problems facing stu-
ts of African urbanization, and certainly among the most
resting.

13

THE CONTINUANCE OF WITCHCRAFT
BELIEFS

by Max Marwick

Many people assume that the African's beliefs in witchcraft are being reduced by his contact with Western culture. This optimism is based on the fact that the civilization into which the African is being drawn is founded on a scientific technology and inspired by a monotheistic religion long since freed from the superstitions underlying a belief in witchcraft.

I am going to suggest that exactly the opposite is true. In the long run an optimistic view may prove to be justified, but it seems to me that the immediate effect of contact with Western influence is not a decrease but an increase in the African's preoccupation with beliefs in magic, witchcraft and sorcery – and for these purposes I include sorcery under witchcraft. Of course this is an hypothesis that cannot be conclusively proved. I am making tentative suggestions rather than reporting on established findings, and I am not going into the question whether anyone actually practises witchcraft; I am concerned with the causes and effects of the belief that there are people who practise it. I should also say that, as a result of my particular experiences and interests, the Africans I am talking about are the East-Central Bantu of Rhodesia and Nyasaland and the South-Eastern Bantu of the Union of South Africa. There is reason to believe, however, that in this matter at least they differ fundamentally from many other African peoples.

I have admitted that I cannot prove my contention that the African's preoccupation with witch beliefs increases as he becomes enmeshed in the modern social system. The first difficulty is that one cannot gauge such preoccupation simply by counting the heads of those who accept the basic belief that certain persons are witches who kill or impoverish their fellow men. In my experience the proportion of people accepting this belief is very high among both educated and uneducated Africans. One of my estimates, based on a small public opinion poll in a Northern Rhodesian rural area, places it between 90% and 100% of the population. But this is a measure of prevalence rather than of preoccupation. It tells us that most people accept the basic witch belief, but it says nothing of the extent to which it preoccupies their minds and worries them. A parallel in our society is the fact that, though we are all aware of the dangers of travelling by car, we vary in the extent to which we worry about the prospect of being killed or maimed in an accident. African witch-anxiety is about as measurable as European accident-anxiety.

The second difficulty is that we cannot speak of increases or decreases in preoccupation with witch beliefs unless we can establish a starting point from which changes are to be measured. There are no records of precisely how witch-ridden Africans were before the coming of Western civilization. We may, of course, ask modern Africans questions such as 'Are there more or fewer witches nowadays than there were long ago?' It so happens that in the tribe I know best the majority of people assert that there are more. But one cannot regard this majority opinion as firm evidence because the tribe I am referring to depict their golden age, the 'long ago' of my question, as a time when the proportion of witches was kept low by the proper and regular administration of the poison ordeal; and they hold this age in glowing contrast to the

degenerate present when, they point out, it is a criminal offen
to accuse anyone of witchcraft, let alone submit him to trial l
ordeal. In other words, because these people tend to ideali
the past – as all societies do – we cannot rely on their compar
tive views of the present.

But having made these qualifications I must explain why –
common, as it happens, with most anthropologists who ha
recorded their impressions in the matter – why I believe th
contact with our civilization does not and will not quick
emancipate the African from his witch beliefs.

In the first place we should not exaggerate the extent
which our own behaviour is influenced by scientific, ratior
thinking; for, although our technology is based ultimately
scientific principles, the proportion of us who have a tru
scientific attitude is very small. We accept the conclusions
our experts as uncritically as primitive men accept the stat
ments of their diviners and medicine men. In short, o
traditional magical beliefs have been displaced more by t
magic of science than by science itself. We may pride oursel\
that our ancestors gave up persecuting witches two and a h
centuries ago, but we retain much of the credulity, supe
stition and cruelty that motivated them; though we m
exhibit these in different fields, such as commercial advertisi
and political persecution. There are still many among us w
believe in astrology, divination by tea-cup, and other practic
quite as irrational as any found in Africa; and in Central ar
Southern Africa itself Bantu diviners are not infrequent\
consulted by white clients.

In view of this it should not surprise us that those Africa
at the very point of contact between the two ways of l
retain firmly rooted beliefs in witchcraft. It is a matter
common knowledge that when it comes to witch beliefs t
labour migrant is often unmoved by his experience of livir

our more secular society; the student impervious to the rational arguments of classroom science; and the convert regretfully resigned to a seventeenth-century type of Christianity that has room for witches. These Africans after all do not come into daily contact with the 'first principles' of our civilization any more than we do. They meet ordinary European people; and in the circumstances of modern Africa their contact with them is in any case somewhat peripheral.

But the main argument involves a slight digression into sociological theory. It is to the effect that an examination of the social functions of witch beliefs in any society suggests that in the society of Africa today – that is, in the situation of culture contact, as it is sometimes called – witch beliefs fall on more fertile soil than they did before the coming of the Europeans.

What is the 'sociology' of witch beliefs in any society, and what are its implications for modern Africa? It is well to remember that during the last thirty or forty years social anthropology, thanks largely to Radcliffe-Brown and Malinowski, has progressed from descriptive ethnography to analytical sociology. There was a time when a social anthropologist was content to make an inventory of the elements, both material and non-material, of the way of life, or culture, of a people. Now he concerns himself primarily with the social significance of these elements. He assumes that each culture-element has a reason for existing, and that this is to be found in the contribution it makes to the effective organization, and ultimately the survival, of the group concerned. When he applies this approach to the study of witch beliefs, he finds that their social function is two-fold. Firstly, they give expression to stresses and strains in the social structure, the network of social relationships linking the members of the group. Secondly, witch beliefs provide occasions for portraying the basic moral principles underlying the social order. If one looks at these two

findings more fully I think it can be shown that, in accordan
with either of them, witch beliefs under the conditions preva
ing in present-day Africa have important functions.

Let us take the structural functions first. Anthropologi
working in a number of societies report that witchcr
accusations are commonest between persons whom the soc
structure throws into opposition and conflict, such as rivals
politics, in love or in work. These accusations periodical
dramatize in the idiom of witchcraft the mutual jealousies ar
irritations of persons in difficult social relationships, and th
serve as important means of purging the social system
destructive tensions. For instance, in many African societi
where polygamy is practised, a man's co-wives often give ve
to their jealousy by accusing each other of witchcraft. A
accusation brings out into the open the underlying causes c
the tension between them, and their husband is thereby giv
the opportunity of making adjustments, such as observing mo
strictly the rule that he should divide his time equally betwe
them. Tension that culminates in witchcraft accusations oft
arises in emotionally-charged situations of this sort, or
situations where mutual rights and obligations are not clear
defined, where there is an element of uncertainty in a soci
relationship. For instance, where inheritance and successic
rules are clear and unexceptionable, there can be no jockeyi
for position; where, on the other hand, they are flexibl
tension and witchcraft accusations are almost sure to mal
their appearance.

A good example of the tension arising from flexibility com
from the Cewa, a matrilineal Bantu people of Nyasalan
Northern Rhodesia and Moçambique. According to the Cev
succession rule, a man's status, for instance a village headmar
ship, passes on his death to the eldest son of his eldest sister; b
the Cewa attach so much importance to personal qualities th

ey frequently disregard this rule if there is any question of
e suitability of the regular heir. So when a man dies it is
ssible for any one of his sisters' sons to succeed him if it can
shown that his rivals are of inferior character. It is not
rprising to find that the uncertainty of this situation often
ds to a mud-slinging contest between rivals. In an African
ciety the most effective means of blackening a rival's character
to accuse him of witchcraft, and nephews competing for
eir deceased uncle's headmanship often resort to this mode of
pressing their tensions.

Why should a witchcraft accusation be an effective kind of
ud-slinging? This introduces the second, or normative,
nction of witch beliefs. Witch beliefs provide the villains for
ociety's morality plays, and thus do much to sustain the body
moral principles that is basic to the social order. To call any-
e a witch is to draw attention, although negatively, to the
ciety's most cherished values, such as humanity, justice and
ciprocity. By depicting the witch as the personification of its
nception of evil, a society forcibly demonstrates its concep-
n of good. In our society, witch-hunts have usually been
sociated with clear-cut religious or political controversies.
argaret Murray has argued that European witches were the
gering adherents of the pagan religion displaced by Christi-
ity. Whether one accepts this interesting hypothesis or not,
e fact remains that the effect of the great witch-hunts at the
ne of the Reformation was to narrow the focus of newly-
nceived Christian objectives and to purge the reform groups
those showing the slightest tendency towards eccentricity
heresy. The leaders of the Reformation, whether in old or
ew England or at Geneva, were able, by calling heretics
itches, to rally to their side a pre-Christian moral indignation.
In modern Africa there are many of the structural tensions
d normative conflicts that we have learned to associate else-

where with witchcraft. Firstly, there are new social alignme
creating insecurity and anxiety. Social, economic and politi
changes, many of them recently accelerated by developm
schemes, bring uncertainty and, from the African viewpoin
dangerous flexibility, to human relationships. Secondly, th
is conflict between modern and indigenous systems of nor
and values – in particular, between the traditional co-operati
of Africa and the individualism of Europe.

Many of the cases of witchcraft accusations that I ha
recorded reflect these tensions produced by modern soc
changes. One finds accusations of witchcraft between fell
workers who are competing for the regard of their employ
between rivals for the inheritance of money earned at work
of property bought with it; between political oppone
jockeying for position in the hierarchy of indirect rule. Whe
ever modern changes have brought about situations for wh
there are no indigenous precedents, and problems for wh
tribal rules of thumb can offer no solutions, these tensions a
and are often expressed in terms of witchcraft.

As to normative conflicts, consider the clash between Chri
anity and the indigenous system of values it seeks to displa
There are, of course, many points of agreement between
general principles of the two systems – presumably because
human moralities have a common core. But the differences
detail, of which the African is probably more conscious, set
convert sharply off from his pagan brethren, and sometin
create tensions between him and them. Take this case,
instance. A young couple – call them John and Edith – l
recently become Christians when John's maternal uncle di
According to tribal custom John should have married his unc
widow, Norma. His acceptance of Christianity made
impossible since it would have involved him in a polygam
marriage. The tension that developed as a result of his refu

was described to me by Edith in these words, 'Norma used to threaten my husband, and I wasn't happy until the day she died'. Before that day arrived, however, two of the children of John and Edith had died, and their deaths had both been attributed to Norma's witchcraft. The implication here is that those who defy the traditional morality do so at their peril.

An outstanding example of the conflict between the co-operation of Africa and the individualism of Europe is to be found in the custom returning labour migrants have developed of entering their home villages under cover of darkness. When asked why they do this, they invariably answer that they are afraid of making their relatives envious of their newly acquired wealth and thus exposing themselves to the dangers of their witchcraft. Now, according to African canons of co-operation they should distribute their wealth among their relatives. But, having chosen the path of European individualism, they do not, and they feel guilty and project their guilt into fears of those whom, by African standards, they have wronged.

It is not surprising that, disturbed by modern social changes, Africans sometimes seek solace in the messianic movements that periodically sweep across large parts of the continent. For our purposes it is significant that many of these movements are directed against witches, who become the symbol of all that is uncomfortable, if not unbearable, in the modern situation.

The proposition that I have offered is that the immediate effect of the African's contact with Western civilization is an increase rather than a decrease in his preoccupation with witch beliefs. I have put forward this view with rather more conviction than is justified by the available evidence, not only because it happens to be my opinion, but also because it is probably less known than the more optimistic, opposed view. It is essential, I think, not to be too strongly committed to either view; for

this is a matter of great practical consequence. The success
government, development and evangelization will depend
some extent on the accuracy of the assumptions we make abo
African incentives. The present-day counter-revolution
racial psychology, which emphasizes equality in the ment
capacity of different races, may incline us to assume that t
incentives that appeal to us appeal also to Africans. But v
should not confuse capacity with contents. Because from ear
childhood Africans are habituated to a culture different fro
ours, they may be expected – in our generation at least –
employ their talents and interests in directions different fro
those in which we employ ours. Development and oth
policies will be misdirected if we ignore this, and particular
if we ignore, or underestimate, the hold of witchcraft belie
Above all the question of incentives is crucial so long as t
African explains illness, crop-failure and industrial accidents
terms of the machination of witches and not as we do in terr
of microbes and misadventure. And so long as his econom
and social advances are accompanied by crippling fears
retaliation from those whom he has left behind, he will partic
pate in development schemes with hesitancy and reservation
if he participates at all.

If my diagnosis is correct, the African is caught in a vicio
circle: his present high degree of preoccupation with wit
beliefs is both a cause and an effect of his difficulty in adjustir
to modern social conditions. Just how long it will take for t
circle to spiral upwards is, like the whole subject of my talk,
matter for debate by those who do not mind inconclusi
findings.

14

THE INDIANS OF NATAL

by Hilda Kuper[1]

is generally accepted in South Africa, not only by politicians,
at the Indian community is 'unassimilable', that it is, and
ways will be, Indian rather than South African, that Indians
tain their traditional way of life unaffected by a Western
ilieu. I think this common judgment is elliptic, even con-
sed. Yet it is worth examining for several reasons, not least
cause it is the basis of the belief – and the policy – that the
dians should be repatriated.

But I do not know if they are 'unassimilable'. That is largely
olitical question, and cannot be answered, obviously, without
amining the desire on the part of the rest of the country to
imilate them; it is after all a reciprocal process. But my study
the Indian community of Natal has made clear to me that
e change of milieu has affected Indian life very much indeed,
r reasons and in ways which are not immediately apparent.
has also clarified why the Indians of Natal have been and still
e so unwilling to be repatriated. South African governments
ve been trying for over 60 years, by every means short of
rect compulsion, to get all Indians except those who were
rving indentures to return to India. Under a voluntary
patriation scheme bonuses of increasing amounts have been
fered, but even these have failed to draw off more than a

[1] At the time of the broadcast Dr Kuper was in Durban as Senior Research
rsar, Institute of Family and Community Health, South African Council for
entific and Industrial Research.

limited number. There is of course a wealthy merchant cla
of people who would face severe financial loss by returnin
but contrary to popular opinion this class is small. The gre
majority of Natal Indians live in extreme poverty, often
conditions worse than the equally impoverished African.

In the whole of the Union there are only 400,000 Indian
most of them living in slum conditions in Natal, and they a
probably more diversified in religion, language, origin an
culture than any other section of South Africa's multi-raci
population. Over 90% of them are South African born, an
many are three-, four- and five-generation South African
About 70% of them are Hindus, 16% Muslims, 6% Christian
and there are Buddhists, Jainists, Zoroastrians, and agnostic
speakers of at least five Indian vernacular languages (Tam
Telegu, Gujerati, Hindustani and Urdu) as well as English an
Afrikaans. There is a small intellectual élite and several thousan
illiterates, a politically sophisticated leadership and a political
untutored mass engulfed in the struggle of daily existence.
small proportion of Indians earn a living as business me
professionals, market gardeners, small-scale planters, and skille
factory hands, but 70% earn a miserable living as semi-skille
and unskilled labourers in agriculture and industry.

Ninety per cent of these people are descendants of imm
grants who came to the country between the years 1860 an
1911 as indentured labourers, in the first place to the sug
plantations, and later to other enterprises. They came i
response to persistent requests for cheap and reliable labou
made by a small group of Europeans, who preceded them i
Natal by less than 40 years. Natal was part of the country
the Zulus, but these were a proud military people who wou
not then, as they do today, accept the inducements of Wester
wages and submit to regular employment by Europeans. Th
indentured came on contract for three and later five years, an

he expiry of their service they could choose either to remain
South Africa as free citizens or to receive a free passage back
India.

t is clear, of course, why they came. Life in India in the
eteenth century was harsh and precarious. Home industries
l decayed with the flooding of the Indian market by British
nufactured goods, the country was overpopulated and the
sants were in need of land. Indenturing offered at least a
ng and in certain cases an escape from difficult domestic
ations. Even so it was not easy to get recruits in adequate
mbers and the extravagant promises of wealth were supple-
nted when necessary by methods commonly known as
olie catching'. One of the legitimate inducements was the
mise of land, equal in value to the return passage to India,
those who stayed on in South Africa. But only a few
ndred received this land, and the promise itself was with-
wn in 1891 when the freed Indians were seen as potential
nomic rivals. They still had the option of a free passage back
India, but the majority chose to remain, and the reasons for
s are really at the root of the entire situation. They chose
remain because even at this early period South Africa had
nged them, and repatriation would have been expatriation.
t is not entirely right though, to put it in that simple,
nsitive way – 'South Africa had changed them'. It is the case
h almost any large movement of peoples that a selective
tor operates. Only certain kinds of Indian came to Natal,
l the resulting body of people did not make a little India.
e shipping and labour records of this period are not very
plicit about the origin of their cargoes, but it has been
ssible to discover a great deal by consulting family traditions
l the memories of old men.

The first indentured came from cities and villages throughout
lia; among them were Dravidians from the south, and the

self-styled Aryans who had invaded them from the north, a
peaceful cultivators and artisans, and warlike men from the hi
But they came into South Africa either as isolated individu
or as isolated families, and even had they so desired they cou
not have recreated in South Africa the variegated and y
interlocking cultural pattern which had been built through t
ages on the Indian continent.

Most of the indentured were Hindus of whom about a fi
only were untouchables, two-fifths were Sudras (labouri
castes), and the rest belonged to the upper or twice-born cast
The nature of the work for which they were recruited and t
conditions under which they lived made it almost impossil
for any but the lowest castes to be again acceptable to th
own village communities, and India itself was not looking f
immigrants. That, coupled with hopes of greater opportunit
in a young, developing country, is largely why most of t
indentured remained in South Africa.

Initially separate from the indentured was a small stream
immigrants distinguished as 'passenger Indians'. They ca
specifically to trade and entered the country under the ordina
immigration laws. Some were wealthy, others had little capit
many were Gujerati-speaking Muslims, and Hindus fro
Bombay Presidency and Kathiawar. These immigrants r
tained contact with their homes through business and marria
but it was in South Africa that they invested their mone
raised their families and spent the greater part of their lives.

The distinction between 'indentured' and 'passenger' und
lies the present economic class structure and accounts f
certain cultural differences, but it is no longer a definite line
cleavage. The economic gap itself has been narrowed by t
emergence from the indentured of a small middle class, a
conversely by the failure of some of the 'passenger' to ret
their economic advantages. More particularly, legislati

ntrolling Indian development induces both sections to unite
their claims as South Africans.

One must go further, and enquire what factors, since the
rly times, have led them to feel that they are a necessarily
uth African community, differing in important ways from
mmunities in India.

Change does not imply rejection or abandonment of one's
ritage, but modification and selective borrowing in the
ocess of adapting to new circumstances. I have mentioned the
rt played by caste in influencing the indentured not to
turn, but it is also very significant that caste no longer
minates and limits the lives of Indians in South Africa.
llution through physical contact was inevitable on the over-
owded ships where 200 to 700 indentured men and women
all castes were squeezed in the 'tween decks for three weeks
three months, fed from a common kitchen and stricken with
e same diseases. In the barracks and shacks where they were
used on their arrival the indentured again shared indiscrimi-
tely the same amenities and the same deprivations. The
aditional elaborate dietary rules fell away almost entirely;
rticipation in communal temple ceremonies, formerly
gulated by caste, became a voluntary personal matter; and it
as the learned or the wealthy, whatever their caste, who
tained responsible positions. Even the symbols of caste soon
sappeared, such as the top-knot and sacred thread of the
wice born'. Caste names lost their former significance and
less they carried high prestige were often abandoned, or
nveniently changed. The specialized hereditary occupations
hich some of these names reflect such as *Teli* – oil presser,
har – smith, were meaningless in South Africa where success
pended on individual achievement, not on claims of caste
periority.

The only caste principle that is still generally recognized is

that of marriage within the caste, and even here other factors
family background, economic standing and education – ma
be considered more important. Moreover, in the early yea
though caste endogamy was the norm, it was almost impossib
to put into practice, for women were indentured in the propo
tion of only 40 to 100 men, and unions across caste barrie
resulted through scarcity not only of women of the right cast
but of women as such.

The only group which adheres rigidly to caste endogan
is the Gujerati Hindu, less than 3% of the total Indian popul
tion, and this adherence flows from their 'passenger' status ar
greater economic freedom. They did not come on the shi
with the indentured and they could afford to bring their wiv
with them or to them. Confronted with the difficulty of findir
the correct mates for their children in South Africa they se
their daughters to husbands in India (since a girl must follo
the domicile of her husband) and imported wives for their son
The Gujeratis are thus the group most affected by Sou
African legislation prohibiting the entry of wives from Indi
and the boys as well as the girls either have to leave the countr
of their birth or follow the general South African India
pattern and admit cross-caste marriages.

The caste units themselves have tended to become larger ar
more inclusive in South Africa, and the vernacular term for
caste is applied to religious groups (Muslims, Christian
Hindus) and to language groups and even to different ethn
groups. These large units, rather than the small tradition
castes, are endogamous, self-conscious and exclusive.

Adherents to caste claim for the system the sanction c
Hinduism, and it is interesting to see how this ancient religic
has adapted itself to the South African environment. Fc
Hinduism in South Africa, as in India, is remarkable for i
absence of rigid dogma and its capacity for absorption c

diverse practices and beliefs. Christianity as an organized religion has little proselytizing appeal, though Christ himself is identified with the beloved Krishna, and incorporated into the Hindu concept of the Divine.

Brahmins were considered unsuitable for indenture, consequently their number was small, and those who came did not represent the spiritual and intellectual élite. Members of non-Brahminic castes began to officiate in essential ceremonies, and Brahmins by entering into mundane life lost their claim to divinity. The religious knowledge of the Hindus deteriorated to such an extent over the early years that in some areas their main public event was the *Muslim* festival of *Moharram* commemorating the murder of the grandson of the Prophet. It was not until after 1900 that occasional Hindu scholars of repute visited the country and instructed the people in the great sacred writings. The masses were ignorant of the literature and philosophy of Hinduism, but they retained many domestic and village rituals. In relation to the size of the population, but reflecting its heterogeneous origin, there is a confusing efflorescence of deities and associated *pujas*.

The situation that broke through caste and influenced the content of Hinduism has also altered the basis of traditional education. Education became secularized. Among the Hindus it broke from the moorings of caste, and among the Muslims it extended beyond the Koran. Education for Indian children in South Africa is neither free nor compulsory, but there are about 300 schools built by Indian effort and subsidized by the Provincial Education Departments. At these schools Western education is imparted through the medium of English to an increasing number of Indian children, of whom a growing proportion are girls. These schools cut across religious and cultural divisions and are probably the strongest levelling influence in the Indian community. Vernacular education

draws fewer children, and while the standard of English :
improving, the Indian languages spoken in South Africa ar
corrupted versions of their originals, often unintelligible t
speakers from India. At the same time many Indians ar
intensely proud of the cultural richness of India, and consider
able influence is exerted on Indians in South Africa by literatur
art, music and films imported from India. The education of th
average South African Indian combines elements of East an
West; but success is measured by achievements not in India bi
in South Africa.

Finally, modifications and resistances inherent in Sout
African conditions are reflected in the family system. A
sections recognize the family as the pivot of social life, th
centre in which the individual receives his basic training i
values and behaviour. It is built on the traditional joint famil
model of three to four generations in which sons live with the
parents after marriage and daughters move to their in-laws.
is, however, becoming increasingly rare to find all the sor
living together after marriage; more usually as a family grow
it subdivides into a number of smaller sections. This divisio
this breakdown of the large consolidated unit, is sometimes th
result of a shortage of accommodation in the parents' hom
but more often subdivision reflects a growing individualis
and independence. Young wives, more particularly if educate
are less prepared to submit to the rule of the in-laws, and th
control of a young man over his own earnings gives him th
opportunity for independence.

Yet the isolated family of man, wife and child is never th
ideal, and suffers recognized social and economic disabilitie
There are very few sons who move immediately on marriag
to a separate dwelling, and while separation may reduce confli
it does not necessarily decrease family obligations. A man is sti
expected to support his parents, assist other poor relation

ducate younger members, help in emergencies and contribute oods and services at numerous ceremonies. Individualism, the mbitious desire for personal success, is considered anti-social nless a man also fully accepts his kinship responsibilities. Many 1en fall into debt through the strain of helping their kin, but t the same time the extended family system is the poor man's 1ain and often sole form of social insurance in South Africa.

The Indians, like the Africans and the Afrikaners, were and re caught in the stream of migration from rural to urban entres, but even under urban conditions the Indian family as proved extraordinarily flexible although subjected to the npact of alien conditions, and to tensions from within. The ery deep economic insecurity of the Indians is partly the eason for this resilience. They have no Native areas and no *latteland* farms where the men can leave their families, and in he migration to the town they must either take their women nd children along or abandon them. To abandon them would iolate their deepest ties, so they take them, and once in the own it is largely because of the women that the Indian family emains as a unit. No matter how poor a family may be the vomen are seldom permitted to seek employment away from ome, for to do so indicates that the men are unable to look fter them properly and the whole family loses prestige. It is he women, especially in Hindu homes, who perform the egular rituals to the domestic deities, bind kinsmen together hrough devotion, and serve as an anchor for the children tossed bout among conflicting values. Even among the educated o skills are more highly rated than those of the housewife, and o rôle is more honoured than that of the mother.

Divorce and illegitimacy rates are lower for the Indian ommunity than for any other ethnic group in South Africa, nd despite poverty, overcrowding and general insecurity, here is relatively little juvenile delinquency and few convictions for serious crimes by adults. But significantly enough, th Indian suicide rate appears to be the highest in the whol country.

I have been speaking about social change among the India community, having dismissed at the start the blunter questio usually raised about their being, or not being, 'assimilable The one matter is very relevant to the other because what ever 'assimilation' might mean it cannot be considered im possible because of any failure on the part of the India community within itself to make adaptations to a South Africa environment.

These changes have come about very largely as a result c external pressures, particularly of course by legislation restrict ing their movement and prohibiting contact with Europeans i any significant way. It is largely as a reaction to segregation tha Indians have preserved, through several hard-pressed genera tions, their cultural inheritance and their unity; and they hav done it, as I have tried to show, by gradual but marked soci and religious modification, responding to a new country to a extent which has been very much under-estimated.

PART TWO

★

15

APARTHEID OR INTEGRATION?

by N. J. J. Olivier

In her racial problem, South Africa is faced with her gravest dilemma and her greatest challenge. It has, especially since the last world war, become of international significance and interest, and rightly or wrongly has been drawn into the cauldron of world politics and the struggle between East and West, between freedom and Communist imperialism. No one in South Africa doubts that the peaceful existence and well-being and prosperity of all our people depend ultimately on a satisfactory solution of this problem.

It is also clear that any solution has to be based on the principles of Christianity, morality and equity, and on the recognition of the basic worth of the human individual; not only because this is right, but because no other kind of solution would be practicable or tolerated.

Because of these considerations I sincerely believe that a policy of *apartheid*, that is, of separate territorial development, provides a possible way out of the dilemma facing the two main groups, European and Bantu.

Before analysing the various policies put forward as an eventual solution to this problem, it is perhaps necessary to state that the present racial situation in South Africa is, of course, the product of a large number of historical factors and forces, which, in conjunction, have brought about the typically South African pattern of race relations and the characteristic (white) South African attitudes and outlook on this matter. Whatever its underlying principles, any solution, or plan, or advice, which does not take into account the facts of this inheritance is, in my opinion, worthless. It is idle to say that history has taken an immoral or 'deplorable' course, and childish to base a theory or a policy on the mere wish that history had taken or will take some other course. The facts are well enough known to everyone, but it is surprising how often they are treated as of no significance: I mean the differences in religion, in civilization and level of development, in physical (racial) characteristics; the military conflict, which led to the imposition of white control over the formerly more-or-less independent Bantu tribes; and the emergence of a South African white nation whose only and exclusive loyalty and love is for this country of its birth.

It is evident that these factors, being a product of history, contain elements both good and bad, beneficial and harmful. I can see no sense in trying to paint the picture in one colour only; I cannot see what good aim is achieved by presenting — South Africa as a slave-state, in which the Bantu population is denied all rights, privileges and opportunities. Such a one-sided presentation is grossly unfair and untrue and cannot succeed in gaining its ends.

On the other hand, it has to be recognized that the present situation, because of its inherent shortcomings, cannot be maintained indefinitely, and has to be changed in some fundamental respects. No society is static, and the growth and development of our Bantu population, their progressive acceptance of Western civilization and way of life, will create growing dissatisfaction and resistance to the restrictions and indignities to which an increasing number of them feel they are being subjected.

South Africa's primary task, therefore, is to decide, without undue delay, on the general direction of her future policy based on the ultimate goal or solution she intends achieving. Radical changes cannot be brought about overnight, but it has also to be accepted that the attainment of the solution will have to be effected within the next few generations; it cannot possibly be postponed for another hundred or two hundred years. As a matter of fact, the time factor is of paramount importance in this whole question.

It is generally conceded by those who think seriously about this problem that there are only two kinds of solution. Either a policy of integration, eventually leading to the creation of a common society consisting of European and Bantu in South Africa, or a policy of separate development, implying the creation of separate 'areas of liberty' (to use the words of the late Prof. Hoernlé) for European and Bantu. There are several intermediate schools of thought, but I cannot conceive of any other alternative providing a solution that is fundamental in character. South Africa will have to choose the one or the other of these two.

This, in fact, is also the conclusion arrived at by the two non-political organizations active in the sphere of race relations in South Africa, namely the South African Institute of Race Relations on the one hand, and the South African Bureau of Racial Affairs on the other.

The South African Institute of Race Relations, formed about 25 years ago, believe, with the South African Liberal Party, that the eventual solution of this problem is to be sought by way of integration and of the creation of a common society. It has, with some direct and indirect overseas financial assistance, advocated this point of view with considerable force. But the white population in South Africa, with the exception of a numerically insignificant minority, has refused to accept the policy put forward by the Institute. I shall later attempt to show why this is so.

The South African Bureau of Racial Affairs, commonly called SABRA, came into existence in 1947. The men responsible for its formation, and generally for its direction and policy consist in the main of Afrikaans academicians and Afrikaans church and cultural leaders. Many have devoted their entire life either to a scientific study of this problem or to the upliftment and development of the Bantu. Their decision to form an organization parallel to the Institute of Race Relations emanated from the sincere conviction that the Institute's approach to these problems could not and would not be acceptable to the overwhelming majority of the white population, and that a solution has to be sought along the lines of a policy of separate development; this principle was formally adopted in its constitution. The existence of these two parallel organizations working in the field of human relations in South Africa is a symptom of the fundamental difference in approach to the solution of this problem.

The final criterion for the judgment as to which of these two alternative policies – integration or separate development – could be successfully applied, is the extent to which a solution for the political problem is provided.

The policy of integration entails the extension of full democratic rights to the Bantu in an integrated political structure, that is, the ultimate removal of any form of differentiation or discrimination between European and Bantu in respect of such matters as voting rights, the right to be elected to all legislative and semi-legislative bodies, the right to be eligible for appointment to all positions in judicial and administrative institutions (including the civil service) and other government or semi-government bodies, the right of access to and use of all public facilities, and so on.

If we were to accept that these changes are to be brought about by democratic means, that is, if we rule out violence and rebellion as a possible means of effecting this equality, it follows that Parliament itself, as the sovereign legislative authority, will have to take the necessary steps, in the form of Acts of Parliament. As regards local government bodies, the various provincial councils will have to enact ordinances to remove differentiation or discrimination as regards, for example, the municipal franchise, membership of municipal councils, and so on.

Now, in the matter of franchise there are, in the main, two possible ways in which such equality may be achieved: the institution of a common voters' roll; or the full application of the principle of group representation (which means the creation of a separate voters' roll for each group, and representation for each group in Parliament). As the latter method is, however, completely rejected even by integrationists, I need not discuss it as a possible solution to the political problem. I myself am convinced that the principle of group representation cannot provide the required solution.

A common voters' roll could be based either on the principle of the universal franchise or on that of the so-called loaded franchise. There is strong difference of opinion amongst integrationists as to whether the franchise is a right or a privilege: if it is regarded as a fundamental right to which all individuals – regardless of economic standing or stage of development – are entitled, it follows automatically that only a system of *universal* franchise could be considered. If, on the other hand, it is to be regarded as a privilege, then the exercise of such privilege could be made dependent on the possession of certain fixed qualifications or requirements.

The universal franchise is the accepted principle in Western democratic countries, and has also been applied in most of the non-white countries where the parliamentary system, based on the franchise, has been introduced.

If, in the particular circumstances of South Africa, the principle of the loaded franchise is advocated, there are two problems to be faced: what the requirements or qualifications are to be; and whether these requirements will apply to Bantu and European alike.

In connection with the first problem the question arises whether the qualifications required for registration as a voter will be such that a fairly large percentage of the Bantu would be able to qualify; for if the system fails to give the greater majority of Bantu some say in the government of the country, the policy itself would be a failure since it would leave substantial numbers of Bantu unrepresented and dissatisfied. The more exacting the qualifications, the less likelihood that they would satisfy the demands and aspirations of the Bantu people.

If the qualifications required are so low that they would satisfy the Bantu generally, then, on the other hand, the result is bound to be – as would be the case with universal franchise – that the majority of the voters will be Bantu.

It seems a fairly safe prediction that, whatever practicable qualifications are required, the eventual result would be that the Bantu voters would outnumber white voters on the common voters' roll. The standard of the qualifications prescribed would only be of importance as to the time when this result will materialize.

Moreover, if the principle of the loaded franchise is accepted for the Bantu, the same principle would have to be applied with regard to the white population, if the accusation of discrimination is to be avoided. In other words, the white population of South Africa, used to the universal franchise for quite a length of time, would have to be prepared to throw this tradition overboard.

Bearing in mind these various considerations, the problem then resolves itself into a very simple question: can it be expected of Parliament, at present representative of the white group first and foremost, to pass legislation which would have the effect of radically curtailing, and possibly even eliminating, the white group's participation in Parliament itself? In other words, is there any foundation for the expectation that the white group, as represented in Parliament, would be prepared to commit political suicide?

I can conceive no greater fallacy than this.

It is evident that the white group will do everything in its power to maintain its right of self-determination, since such right is a prerequisite to its national existence. It is also clear that a policy aimed at depriving the South African white nation of its inalienable right of self-determination is unfair and unjust, and consequently fails to meet the requirements I stated at the beginning.

In reply to this, the argument is sometimes put forward that the white group ought to, and perhaps may, be prepared to extend its concept of nationhood to include the Bantu, so that a new South African multi-racial nation would come into existence. Apart from the fact that this argument confuses cause with effect, it is much more probable that future events will produce the opposite result: the tensions and conflicts caused by a policy of integration will be such that the peaceful emergence of a single multi-racial nation can, as a practical possibility, be ruled out. Why have the nations of Western Europe maintained their existence as separate national entities? The Irish in the Irish Free State rejected a common nationhood with the people of the United Kingdom; the same is true of Pakistan and India; of Israel and the Arabs; of Tunisia, Morocco and France; of the Sudanese and Egypt. And when one considers how far removed are the whites in South Africa itself from complete unity, between the English and Afrikaans-speaking sections, there appears to be small justification for the hope that a single multi-racial nation will emerge in South Africa.

I believe that it is basically wrong and unfair towards the Bantu population to hold out a promise of futue non-differentiation and equality, when I know full well that the possibility of it barely exists.

What I have said about the likelihood of a parliamentary voters' roll based on the principle of non-discrimination, applies with equal force to the various other aspects I have mentioned. Is it possible to visualize that in the foreseeable future the Bantu will be allowed to enter and compete in the civil service on a footing of equality with whites? Is it possible to conceive of a time when South Africa may have a Bantu as Secretary, say, of Agriculture, or of Finance, or of Internal Affairs? That a Bantu will sit as magistrate or judge deciding cases where all parties are whites? That they will have and exercise the municipal franchise in the same way as whites do, and possibly control, say, the Johannesburg City Council? That they will be allowed to acquire ownership in land wherever they want to? That they will be allowed to reside wherever they feel inclined to?

It is not a question of the Bantu being innately incapable of performing various functions within an integrated society or filling responsible posts. On the contrary, there is nothing to suggest that, given education, training and experience, they cannot do these things with dignity and competence. Neither is it a question of the white man being inherently superior or suffering from an irrational colour prejudice. The truth, pure and simple, is that continued existence of white nationhood precludes developments of this kind in an integrated society.

Territorial and economic integration of white and Bantu is therefore bound to lead to growing frustration on the part of the Bantu, and increasing measures on the part of the white population to maintain its dominant position and safeguard its existence. This will to an ever-increasing extent be interpreted as oppression of the Bantu, and will give rise to strains and conflicts of unpredictable seriousness and magnitude within this society.

On these grounds we are compelled to reject a policy of integration as a possible solution to this problem.

I believe that if the white group in South Africa feels itself justified to resist any policy that may jeopardize its right of political self-determination, it has the moral duty and obligation not to deny that right to others. I believe also that the white group in the legitimate exercise of this right, should not, need not, and would not act in such a way that it could be accused of oppression, of being immoral and unjust.

The only possible course open to us, if we were not to demand the supreme sacrifice of the European or of the Bantu group, if we want to co-exist in a spirit of brotherly love and co-operation, is that which provides for the separate political development of each, the creation of separate 'areas of liberty'.

Quite naturally the question arises: where, how and when is this going to be effected?

The existing Bantu areas in the Union of South Africa will naturally have to serve as a nucleus for this development. These areas comprise at the moment almost forty million acres, almost two-thirds the size of the United Kingdom. The High Commission Territories would probably in course of time become an integral part of the whole scheme. Some people maintain that planning on a Southern Africa regional basis will have to take place, but this, of course, could only be done in co-operation with the Union's northerly neighbours. Depending on their response the future extension of our own Bantu areas might have to be considered.

These areas will have to be developed to the extent that they

can provide a domicilium for the majority, if not fo
practically all, of our Bantu population. This entails the large
scale development, industrialization and urbanization of th
Bantu areas on the lines suggested by the Tomlinson Com
mission. The guiding principle should be that these areas shoul
become the national home for the Bantu, in which progressiv
development towards political self-determination should tak
place.

I believe this could be done without dislocation of ou
economy, and that the white population will be prepared t
make the economic sacrifices required for the full implementa
tion of this policy.

I know that it is almost impossible for people living outsid
South Africa to understand the South African situation, and i
general to agree with the course that the white man in Sout
Africa is compelled to pursue. As a matter of fact, we do no
expect nor ask for such agreement. What we do expect, and
think are entitled to ask, is a sympathetic understanding of th
dilemma facing the various groups in South Africa, and a littl
compassion also for the white population in the giganti
problem which, largely without its choice, it is called upo
to face.

16

APARTHEID OR INTEGRATION?

by Ellen Hellman

apartheid, as everyone knows, is the progeny of the National Party. Assiduously tended by the Native Affairs Department and nurtured in the congenial environment of South Africa's traditional policy of segregation, the infant has grown prodigiously. But one abnormality the child did develop in its rapid growth: it became hydra-headed and, though it speaks with an assurance and a fluency far beyond its nine years of age, the fact that it speaks simultaneously with these many tongues certainly detracts from its clarity of expression.

Non-whites are, understandably, less intrigued by the babel of voices than are the whites, and less inclined to debate the precise shade of meaning to be attributed to this or that voice. To them *apartheid* has meaning in terms of certain acts passed by Parliament, certain regulations promulgated, certain discretionary powers exercised by cabinet ministers. To them it means a Group Areas Act and a Natives Resettlement Act, tighter control of African entry into the towns, refusal of passports, immobilization and muzzling of elected leaders. To them it has the most immediate of meanings in terms of regulating where they may or may not live and trade, what work they may do, where they may travel. To some few it also means advantages which derive from a reduction of the area of competition, as did the system of segregation in the United States.

To the whites *apartheid* has varying meanings, dependin upon which of its differing countenances their gaze is fixed. T some, but extremely few, *apartheid* means eventual partition a division of South Africa into two or more completel independent states. With India, Ireland, Palestine as thei models, they see in the creation of a *Bantustan* for the African the only possibility of relieving racial pressures in the Unio But these are individuals, largely inarticulate, their ideas rejecte by the overwhelming majority on the grounds of danger a much as of impracticability.

Those who interpret *apartheid* to mean a territorial separatio stopping short of complete independence have a larger follow ing, particularly among the Afrikaans intellectuals and th ministers of the Dutch Reformed Church. They form however, a numerically insignificant minority despite th intellectual and moral prestige attaching to some of thei leaders. Largely this school of thought expresses itself throug SABRA, the South African Bureau of Racial Affairs, which like the older established South African Institute of Rac Relations, was set up to promote racial concord. But wherea the Institute commenced in 1929 with no pre-conceive doctrine, SABRA's aims from its inception in 1947 specificall laid down that such concord shall be brought about on th basis of the separate development of each racial group. SABR stands for this: 'The territorial separation of European an Bantu, and the provision of areas which must serve as nation and political homes for the different Bantu communities'. order to reconcile the conflicting necessities of reducing th permanent Bantu population in the so-called white areas to minimum and ensuring a sufficiency of African labour for th 'European' economy, greater use is to be made of migrar workers. As far as political rights are concerned, the fin answer is left to the future. The fears of those who see territori

eparation leading to the creation of a potentially hostile
utonomous Bantu state are countered by the assurance that
Europeans will continue to exercise a measure of control in the
Bantu areas for a long time, that not one but a number of
Bantu areas are visualized, and that some form of federation
nay by then be possible.

By and large these are also the objectives to which the
Government itself purports to be directing policy. Dr
Verwoerd, the Minister of Native Affairs, says that '*Apartheid* is
 process of continually increasing separation in all the spheres
f living, and this takes place even when there is no territorial
eparation. . . . The logical end of continually increasing
partheid in the social, economic and political fields is indeed
erritorial separation, but no one can foretell when that point
vill be reached.'

On paper the difference between the Government's policy,
vhich goes under the name of 'practical *apartheid*', and the
chool of territorial separation may not appear to be great.
But in fact there is so considerable a difference in emphasis and
n practical intent as to make them two different policies. The
atter group urges the immediate introduction of practical
neasures to start implementing territorial separation, no matter
vhat the cost. It is fully conscious of the sacrifices Europeans
vill have to make in capital to develop the Native Reserves,
nd in labour to replace the present ready supply of African
vorkers in home and factory. Few government spokesmen
are speak in this vein. In the main they agree with Dr Malan,
vho said that for the foreseeable future territorial separation is
imply not practical politics. It is true that the Government is
ttempting to restrict further permanent urban African settle-
nent by preventing wives and children from joining their
nenfolk in towns and thereby deliberately increasing the
roportion of migrant workers. But it is not, for very obvious

political reasons, prepared to take its policy of restricting entry to the towns to the lengths of depriving existing industries of their labour or of preventing new industries from being established. Both Dr Verwoerd and Mr M. C. de Wet Nel, a member of the Native Affairs Commission, have said that the number of Africans coming into the European areas and working in the European economy would increase before the stream started flowing the other way. What this amounts to is a type of *apartheid* which allows economic integration to continue which allows the economic and territorial intermixture of white and black, and concentrates on bringing about increased residential separation, increasing separation in public amenities and social services and preventing social contacts in any form. This is precisely the form of *apartheid* which SABRA, while refraining from attacks on the Government, in fact condemns. This amounts, it considers, to sacrificing the white man's heritage for the sake of immediate gain.

To most Europeans, however, whether they be Afrikaans or English-speaking, supporters of the National or United Parties, *apartheid* has come to mean no more and no less than preserving the *status quo*, which accords certain privileges to all whites. Of course, the desire to retain established privileges is not peculiarly South African failing. Further, most Europeans in the Union consider this order of society essential to preserve their way of life, to ensure the perpetuation of European culture. Outnumbered as they are by four to one, with close on nine million Africans out of a total population of less than thirteen and-a-half million, with immense cultural differences within the African population and large numbers illiterate and close to their tribal state, it is understandable enough, even if not scientific and rational, that fear should pervade the European community. There is the fear of sheer numbers, fear that if the barriers of racial separation are not fortified, the European will be obliterated as a distinctive racial group, that waves of barbarism will sweep away what is generally known as 'white civilization'.

Until very recently one of the main justifications for segregation was the alleged obligation of the white man, as the dominant element, to preserve the fabric of Bantu culture and to allow the African to develop on his own lines. Implicit in this approach, even if seldom explicit, was the assumption that the African is inherently incapable of assimilating Western culture. Dr Malan gave expression to this very prevalent pattern of thought when he said that 'the difference in colour is merely the physical manifestation of the contrast between two irreconcilable ways of life, between barbarism and civilization, between heathenism and Christianity'. Dr Malan is of course correct when he says that the two ways of life – Bantu tribalism and Western industrialism – are irreconcilable. The immense changes that have taken place in Bantu culture, continually accelerating in tempo and bringing about the ever greater disintegration of tribalism, show that the two systems cannot co-exist. But to say, as Dr Malan does, that 'the racial differences are as pronounced today as they were three hundred years ago' flies in the very face of existing reality. The colour differences certainly do still exist. But the cultural differences are being bridged, slowly, unevenly but quite unmistakably. What Dr Malan did was to equate colour and culture. This equation underlies much of South African thinking.

The Report of the Commission on Native Education, from which was born the highly controversial Bantu Education Act, does not go as far as Dr Malan, nor adopt as static an approach. It concedes that the subjection of Africans to European political and economic control 'has made the smooth functioning of the original social institutions, such as the family and the tribe, a matter of increasing difficulty'. It is nevertheless insistent that there must be a Bantu education, as distinct from other kinds of education, to develop a distinctive Bantu culture. It consider that 'the old traditional Bantu cultures contain in themselve the seeds from which can develop a modern Bantu culture full able to satisfy the aspirations of the Bantu and to deal with th conditions of the modern world'. Bantu education must promot Bantu culture, the Report says, it must provide for a Bantu chil trained and conditioned in Bantu culture, endowed with knowledge of a Bantu language, imbued with the values, interest and behaviour patterns learned at the knee of a Bantu mother

The contradiction in this approach is, I submit, obvious On the one hand it concedes the necessity for imposing Western economic and political institutions and recommend the provision of schools with a definite Christian character an adequate social institutions to harmonize with such schools; ye on the other hand it rejects schools of a Western type becaus they do not reinforce the social institutions of Bantu societ but transmit ideas, values, attitudes and skills which have no been evolved in Bantu society itself.

It is an anthropological truism that social institutions form a interrelated whole: and that when one institution is changed this sets off a series of changes which ramify throughout th culture. This is precisely what is happening to Bantu culture. is clear that the vast majority of Africans are directly dependen on the 'European' economy for their livelihood and ar accordingly required to learn and perform new skills an conform to an entirely new set of working conditions, whic include insistence on regularity of work, punctuality, a impersonal authority structure and a different set of incentive The values, attitudes, skills deriving from Bantu culture are no only unsuitable in the context of a Western economy: they ar obstacles preventing the aspirant African worker from gettin and holding the job he needs.

The incorporation of the African into Western economy has had far-reaching effects on family structure and relationship patterns. In both town and country families are becoming smaller. Recent surveys have shown an average of a fraction over five persons per family. Increasingly the elementary family, consisting of mother, father and children is coming to be the normal residential unit and not, as was formerly the case, a homestead comprising a group of relatives. The geographical isolation from kin and tribe of the elementary family, one among thousands of similar units drawn from all areas of the Union and beyond, is weakening both kinship and tribal bonds. They are coming to be superseded by bonds based upon neighbourhood and common interests. The immense proliferation of associations – religious, economic, recreational, philanthropic, occupational – among urban Africans is evidence of the new structure that is taking shape.

Behaviour patterns within the family are changing. The old principles of respect for seniority and male dominance are being modified by the new values attaching to educational attainment and wealth. The necessity for women to contribute to family income because most of the men do not earn enough, is giving women higher status and greater independence. This, together with the influence of Western patterns transmitted through contact in the form of domestic service, through books, magazines and films, is making the husband-wife and parent-child relationships less authoritarian and more democratic. On the other hand, the opportunities open to the individual to support himself and to free himself completely of family obligations, are undermining family cohesion. The church, the school, sports clubs, public entertainments have, as among Europeans, taken over many of the functions formerly fulfilled by the family. In short, the direction of development is towards increasing adaptation to Western patterns. The rapidly increasing African middle class, in its clothes and household furnishings, in its recreation and entertainments, its religiou practices and educational striving and, above all, in its aspira tions, clearly illustrates the extent of acculturation. Significantly enough, the degree of Westernization is in itself one of the important attributes of middle-class membership.

Throughout Africa there is a pull between traditional politica institutions, particularly chieftainship, and Western democrati institutions. In South Africa, where contact has taken place ove a longer period than elsewhere and the functions of the chie have been more restricted, the aim of organized Africar political movements is to abrogate the old system and to participate in the country's Western governmental system Tribal loyalties are being increasingly submerged by nationa loyalties built up in the common struggle for freedom. Though the Government, through the Bantu Authorities Act, is trying to build up the power of the chiefs and restore a Bantu aristocracy, new conditions will inevitably compel modifica tions of the institution of chieftainship. One illustration is the proposed establishment of rural towns in the Reserves. These towns are to consist of half-acre freehold plots – a system o tenure completely alien to and incompatible with the tradi tional system. Once the development of the Reserves is actively undertaken, there will necessarily be ever greater departure from tribal relationships, tribal standards of behaviour, triba values. The accent will be, as it increasingly is in the urbar areas, on individual initiative, individual effort, private property. If modern agricultural practices are adopted – and particularly if there is industrial employment – it is mos improbable that a hereditary chieftainship assisted by appointed councillors will be able to maintain itself.

In fact, official emphasis on the preservation of traditiona Bantu culture has grown much less of recent years. The schoo f territorial separation sees clearly that present economic evelopments are lessening cultural differences and that unless his process is halted European political leadership will be ndangered.

This is the point where territorial separation, the Government's practical *apartheid*, and the desire of the common man to preserve what is, find common ground. All, except the few isolated partitionists, are united in their determination to retain exclusive white political control. The long fight over the Coloured franchise in the Cape was fought not on the issue of the right of the Coloured voter to remain on the common roll, but on the issue of the unconstitutional means adopted to effect its removal. There is, admittedly, growing recognition of the changes taking place in Bantu culture. But this has not led to a greater preparedness to integrate non-whites into the full range of Western institutions. On the contrary, it appears that something in the nature of a defence reaction has been provoked and that there is a greater determination to enforce separation where it is possible: namely politically and socially. It seems to me extremely unlikely that this attempt can succeed for any length of time in face of the economic and social forces at work in the Union. Such success as is apparently attending the present policy of increasing separation is, I believe, illusory: for behind the façade of *apartheid*, immense sociological and economic changes are forging ever more indestructibly the bonds of inter-dependence between white and black. They are creating the conditions which must, I am convinced, bring into being not separate racial societies, but one shared multi-racial community.

PART THREE

★

17

THE AFRICAN INTELLECTUAL

by Ezekiel Mphahlele

he first thing to say about the African intellectual, at any rate
the Union, is that the wider setting against which he must be
nderstood is almost precisely the same as that of the non-
tellectual. In fact it may not differ very much from that of the
on-literate. By 'setting' I mean broad and basic things such as
s origins, family background, where he lives and how well he
ves. His personal history differs of course, and his view of
mself, and the view which others take of him. Sometimes,
y no means always, his daily occupation differs.

Consider first his family background. There are many who
me of families educated and established for two or more
nerations in the towns; but if not he, then his father or grand-
ther, was a man who came from a tribal community which
d never experienced the need for formal schooling in the
estern sense. In the process of time this man gets caught up in
e stream of an industrial revolution or a European farming
onomy that goes beyond the ordinary subsistence level of his
mmunity. Because he is not allowed to buy land except from
all released areas he finds himself compelled to leave the now
id and over-populated Reserves.

He drifts to the towns to seek work so that he may pay his
xes and levies and feed his dependants, who remain scratching
r a living on poor soil in the Reserves. He must understand
s employer's instructions in English or Afrikaans, read names
streets and shops. He feels utterly inadequate in this respect,

and he begins to realize how vital education is to the needs o
his kind.

It all starts as an economic weapon – this going to schoo
But it is also because of this economic aspect that most Africa
children leave school after four school years. They must go o
and augment the family income.

However, with more and more Africans going on to hig
school and to university the cultural function of education h
begun to assume higher and universal standards. The econom
yardstick is no longer adequate, and the 'intellectual' emerge
by which I simply mean a class of men who are interested :
cultural matters for their own sake, and for their relevance
affairs beyond the individual's own immediate personal goo

My own 'case-history' is that I was born in the slums
Marabastad, in Pretoria. When I was seven we moved to th
Northern Transvaal and I herded goats and cattle, and when
wasn't harvest or hoeing time I attended school. When I w
thirteen we moved back to Pretoria, where I was able to atten
school regularly. Outside school hours I carried washing for m
mother to and from whites in the suburbs. Somehow w
managed that I went to high school, and I got a scholarship fe
a teacher's course. I was a schoolteacher for fifteen years, ar
during that time I took a B.A. Honours degree in English b
private study, and am now working on a thesis for an M.
degree. I no longer teach, but work as a journalist and write

But except that I have these interests and was to this exte
able to pursue them, I, and the many like me, come from th
same kinds of home, and live now under the same uncerta
conditions and in the same way as our fellow African town
men. We are very much affected by the constant movement
our people, either by government order, or force of econom
circumstance, or the shortage of housing which compe
people to move out of townships to squat on open land.

There are many ways, however, in which the intellectual is really worse off than others. In a life of so much frustration, and conditions that place even the basic things out of reach, the masses look up to the educated man to lift them out of the bog. They expect him to win for them political and financial power. The intellectual has not lived up to these expectations. Things have not been easy. Before industry started to employ a considerable number of Africans, the teacher's salary, low as it was – six pounds a month – was above that paid to unskilled workers. So was the clerk's. Today the workers have climbed up to skilled and semi-skilled jobs and their wages exceed those of the teacher and clerk. Again, because most intellectuals are in government employ or that of state-subsidized private agencies, they have not been able to do much for the masses for fear of victimization, and the loss of even the little they earn. And now the masses are disillusioned: even the village schoolmaster does not enjoy the wholesome respect that his predecessor did.

It is a lonely man who is not taken seriously by his own people, yet cannot keep aloof from them and their daily miseries.

The teaching profession is the most common among educated Africans. The teacher's course is not long – three years if one takes it after the primary school Standard 6; two years if one had done a three-year course in high school. An African may also become a doctor: a most expensive undertaking, unless he decides to swallow his pride by accepting a scholarship to the one and only medical school the government has set up specially for non-Europeans.

One may be a traffic inspector. But only very few cities and towns employ African inspectors. There are only forty such inspectors in Johannesburg. There is also the job of assistant librarian. But municipal libraries are a negligible number.

There are few openings for social work, and the only school o
social work for Africans in South Africa produces abou
eighteen graduates every year. The demand for social worker
slightly exceeds the supply, but the salaries offered are mos
unattractive. Outside these spheres the intellectual can only b
a clerk, and forget about a career. There are many such peopl
who have decided to doff their professional garments and g
into industry to do manual work or as drivers.

The fact is that white industrialists and lawyers do not wan
an African worker who is 'too educated'. They are content if a
worker can read and write, speak English intelligibly an
understand instructions of the simplest kind. They are incline
to suspect the highly educated worker.

A year ago I worked in a Jewish lawyer's office as a messenger
clerk. I am able to do touch-typing, and I used to help his whit
typist. Now one day, as I had often done before, I was using a
typewriter facing the counter in the reception compartment
My employer tapped me on the shoulder and called me to hi
office.

'You'll have to carry your machine into the waiting-room
where you make tea,' he said. 'You see, my white clients wil
rave mad if they see a black man near the reception counter
Please remove it at once.'

He wanted my services, but not at any price. He liked my
hands and brain, but not my face. But he had to keep me be
cause if he hired a white man to do the same work as I did, h
would have to pay him twice as much.

The intellectual is clearly not wanted in the city. He i
regarded as a creature that always gets in the way, if not a
positive menace. The whites prefer illiterates or semi-literates
who accept their humble station; who can run down and bu
sandwiches, or a bunch of flowers for the typist, and sometime
a packet of cigarettes for her boy-friend. It must be the humbl

ort who accepts a tickey or left-overs from the typist's lunch
with a grateful grin, and who goes about the premises like a
rained animal.

A humiliating rôle for anybody, according to the degree of
ensitivity. There are certain people who have been hardened
by the necessity to keep a job. They may be called 'Jim' or 'boy'
by a shop assistant and keep calm. They know that if they
llowed themselves to lose their temper every time they were
hus insulted, life under the white man would be perpetual pain.
But there are some of us whose pitch of sensitivity is always
igh and does not allow such a philosophic acceptance of the
osition.

It is not uncommon even for an African university graduate
to be without work for which he is qualified. If he does get
uch work, then in common with other educated men,
raduate or non-graduate, he receives only two-thirds or even
half of the wages of the semi-skilled worker of his race in, say,
he building industry, or in the factory or a driver's job. And
aturally he wonders if all his study has been worth his while.
Often he dares not reveal his educational qualifications to a
rospective employer or his boss. He must remain tacitly
pologetic about his educational status. Meantime, he owes it to
is people and himself to acquit himself well.

Two factors baulk the educated African's efforts: his colour
nd what is known in South Africa as the 'civilized labour
olicy'. The African's rival in this country is the kind of white
worker – of about 18 to 35 years of age – who comes from the
ountry, usually without a high school certificate. His counterpart in the city, the poor white, is an equally serious rival. In
ach case it is the European youth who has made a failure of
cademic schooling who is enabled to take up a job as a shop
ssistant, store-keeper, post office clerk, municipal location or
ther public service clerk, laboratory assistant, foreman an so

on – all the posts which, as things are, the African university
graduate might be glad to get.

Government officials and educationists have been complain-
ing that European technical colleges have been producing
very poor workers who either fail their examinations or make
inefficient apprentices. Another complaint is that too few white
do the matriculation. The reason is, surely, that there is alway
sheltered employment for white youths and knowledge of thi
is no incentive to hard work.

What about the educated man's prospects of a job among
Africans, in the locations? My people have been a reservoir fo
the white man's cheap labour for so long that all too few o
them can become economically independent of the white
employer. It is true that the authorities do not allow any othe
racial group than Africans to own shops in municipal locations
But they are mostly grocer shops, and butcheries. There ar
very few other trades, because it is difficult to start withou
capital or training. In a Johannesburg township, the larges
African location in the southern hemisphere with a popula
tion of 100,000, there is only one printer; there is one plumber
one African and six European medical doctors (who have
special licence to practise here). There is one high school; on
social centre; one post office. There are only two small clinic
There are no bakeries, abattoir, or market, or departmen
stores or factories, or life insurance or estate agents' offices; n
commercial school, no men's hostel. There are no chemis
shops, no stationery or drapery shops; no cinema or beaut
salon; no park.

Now all these essentials would provide skilled and semi
skilled as well as unskilled work in the African urban area
But when the intellectual has been virtually forced out of th
white man's town, he falls back on a poor community tha
cannot use his services.

This brings me to the irony of the whole position. The African is continually told by whites, and by the Government: 'You do not belong in the city. This is white man's land. Of course if you have come to work for us, you're welcome. By all means rent a house in the location. But if you were not born here, or if you have not been working for at least 15 years continuously in this district, you must go to the Reserves, where you were born, and where you really belong. Even if you're not redundant, you've got to get this clear in your mind: you can't get the municipal vote. Besides, there are no high-grade jobs for you here. That's the white man's field.

'Why don't you go back and serve your own people? We'll give you local councils to govern yourselves in your townships – under white supervision, of course, until you've mastered the tricks of the trade. You're wondering what you'll do in the Reserves? There's work there for everyone who wants to work. We know the land is in a bad state, but the government is doing all it can to restore and conserve soil and water. Tell your people they're in for a time of prosperity in the near future. They'll soon be getting industries brought right to their doorstep. You'll soon have your own cities, with cinemas, theatres, swimming baths, parks, technical colleges, doctors, engineers and what-have-you. Just as the Europeans have in their own areas. These things take time, and you'll mar everything from the start if you agitate the minds of your people by telling them to demand parliamentary or municipal government. You know most of them don't care for such big things. They're still backward. . . .'

That's what the African is told. But he knows not only that the promised Eldorado in the Reserves is too good to be true, but that if it were feasible, it would amount to an incalculable loss to his own people. It would mean that the black man must forsake the cities to which his labour has contributed so much and turn to building for a dream state. It would also mean a sad break with friends he has made among whites and some of the excellent things in their culture. He resents being told to cut his suit according to his cloth, when he has been given moth-eaten material or none whatever.

As a group, intellectuals are too unsettled and insecure to take up a vanguard position in the cultural development of their people. They are men with white collars and empty pockets.

It is obvious that the higher a man goes in educational attainment the more demands he makes for his spiritual and material comfort. He may want to own a radio set, or a gramophone and good music records; he may want to attend a lecture or cinema in town; he may be a book collector; he may want free access to public libraries in town. He wants a bigger house, respectable dress and he wants to eat better: and these are gnawing demands.

It is against this platitude that the argument becomes even more stupid that the white man has a higher standard of living – inherently so – which must be perpetually buoyed up at the expense of the African worker. In any case, both black and white pay the same price for goods in the shop.

What does the intellectual think of the policy of *apartheid*? He finds partial *apartheid* annoying because it cripples him. And he is not enchanted with the idea of total *apartheid*, especially when he is now being told that migrant labour will continue to form an integral part of the country's economy, which can mean nothing less than perpetual inequality.

The bulk of African *traders*, in the townships, are eager to help the government bring about total segregation, because they think this will ensure a monopoly of trade, unhindered by the entry of Indians, Coloured and Europeans. But as only a negligible number of traders are to any extent educated, they have nothing to lose by being cut off from the hub of intellectual life, having few or no cultural pursuits.

The future is a gloomy one. There are a number of things African intellectuals have conceded and tried to be philosophic about. Very few dream of 'Africa for Africans'. Most of them think in terms of a South African population of Africans, Indians, Coloureds and Europeans. They have also made tremendous strides in bringing together the various tribes into a black national unit, and they resent the present system of tribal grouping the State is enforcing in their townships, which sets the process back.

In the same way the cultural bridges whereby we could get together with Europeans who have like aspirations are being broken down. We fear that if this trend of South African politics continues – which is to bottle up races in small distinct entities – then the country is heading for a possible clash between two nationalisms, which will mean a switch back to something like the Cape Eastern Frontier clashes between black and white during the eighteenth century.

Some people, in South Africa and abroad, would say that white segregationists are sincere people who want to find a Christian solution to a problem peculiar to a so-called multi-racial society. But the African intelligentsia feel that if the white man were sincere he would consult the African about his plans – in fact they would plan together – instead of continually thrusting systems of education, ethnic grouping, residential segregation and so on down his throat with the implication: 'You may not like this, but you must like it.'

I believe that to most intellectuals, white leadership or Christian trusteeship has become a chimera. We regard it as dishonest. For that matter, the Christian faith has lost its original enchantment, because it seems to us that it has become the very expression of the dishonesty of the West. We have become disillusioned in missionary teaching, because while we were being evangelized and taught to tolerate our oppressor, very little if any similar evangelizing was being done among the whites. Missionary teaching may have been good for its own sake, but it has become inadequate in a South African context because, as it seems to many of us, it adopts an outworn, orthodox, and even reactionary approach to intricate political problems.

The African intellectual is prepared to live with the white man. But he asks for no paternal benevolence. He wants justice: a universal justice. The text for a South African sermon will always be the one given by Mr Adlai Stevenson when he ended his visit here: 'Be just to your neighbour and let God take care of the rest.'

18

THE INDIAN OUTLOOK

by Somarsundarum Cooppan

I speak as an Indian who was born in South Africa, and has lived all his life in a city. Some 95% of the Indians in the Union are South African-born, and about 70% of us live in areas classified as urban; so I am not in any way unusual.

For the many Indians who, like myself, are in the fourth generation South African, the links with India are tenuous. Of course, there is a sentimental attachment to India, somewhat like the sentiment of Englishmen in the Dominions. Living in a society dominated by Western culture to a far greater extent than India itself, South African Indians have made selective adaptations to their environment and the process of acculturation does not stop. I think we have grown so accustomed to living in a Western milieu that we would feel unhappy out of it.

We think and express ourselves best in English. We aspire to what is called a Western standard of living. That is where some of our difficulties arise, for obviously we need better jobs, higher levels of income, education and technical training to come anywhere near our aspirations.

You will understand that in common with the other non-European peoples of the Union, the Indians are fundamentally affected by racial segregation. To all of us segregation means discrimination against us in every aspect of life, and confines us to a status of permanent inferiority. There is no tradition or even pretence of providing separate facilities that are also equal. The country, of course, simply could not afford the cost. In the field of employment what used to be largely a matter of conventional discrimination is now a law, which enables the Minister of Labour to reserve certain classes of employment for certain racial groups. You may say that this is a caste system to which Indians ought to be accustomed. Yes, it is. Except that in India it is being legislated out, and in Christian South Africa it is being carefully perpetuated.

The white man in South Africa, for all his power, is constantly aware that he is a member of a minority group. There are some, especially among the Afrikaners, who become quite frenzied if the colour bar is relaxed ever so little.

Now, the Indian community forms a much smaller minority than the European; only about 410,000 in a total population of about 13,000,000; and we have no power at all. We have no vote in central, provincial or municipal government, and no indirect representation either, as the Africans have. You may wonder, then, whether Indians show the same 'minority' attitudes and fears as the white group, and what in general our relationship is both to the whites and to the great African majority.

With regard to the whites, our fears of course are fundamental and may be obvious. It is claimed that there is a positive aspect to the *apartheid* policy, that of developing the so-called Bantu areas or Native Reserves into economically viable homelands for the African people. Whether one is impressed by this or not, it remains that this positive aspect does not apply to Indians. White men decide what is good or bad for Indians, and the white man does not even claim that he is going to 'develop' us. In fact he wants to be rid of us, by 'repatriation', back to India, as though that were where we belonged. It may be noted, however, that in her dispute with India, South Africa claims that Indians are South African nationals, and that the United Nations Assembly therefore has no jurisdiction over the treatment of Indians.

The so-called positive aspects of *apartheid* do not apply to us, but all the negative ones do. Very few people, even among white South Africans, know that the Indian is condemned to live and die in the province in which he was born. He cannot go and take up a job in a neighbouring province, and even to go for a holiday he needs a special travel permit. This was the case even before the *apartheid* legislation. Now, under the Group Areas Act, life for Indians will be constricted even more, for not only must they reside in the locations or group areas set aside for Indians, but they must also trade there, taking in one another's washing, as it were. This segregation is to be now applied in provinces and cities which did not do this sort of thing before.

We do not believe that all white South Africans are behind the present system. A few have been putting up a valiant battle for justice and fair play. Much of the educational and hospital services which non-whites have today are due to their efforts. Canon Collins said in South Africa that many of those whom he had met would be happy to wake up and see the colour bar and its iniquities gone. But who dares to take the lead? The Liberal Party of South Africa is trying to mobilize these forces in the white fold into a politically conscious and active group. The party even accepts non-whites to its membership. The Liberal Party is, however, under fire from all other white parties, and the process of winning over the white electorate promises to be slow, too slow for those of us who have to bear the brunt of racial discrimination. Consequently the Liberal Party is regarded by many non-white political leaders as a diversionist group, likely to delay the non-white liberatory struggle.

The tragedy of the whole situation is that white discrimination has produced in reaction a similar kind of intolerance against the whites. A growing number of non-white educated individuals are not prepared to make any distinction between the sincere, progressive, liberal-minded white men, and the rabid racialists. Such people no longer believe in the *bona fides* of the white man. The worst swear word in the non-white political world is 'Collaborator'. There is still a broad band of non-white leadership which has not allowed itself to become embittered, and agitates for a dignified partnership with the white man. White men in South Africa do not appear to be prepared for this step. Therefore, the different sections of the non-white people see no other way out but to get together and fight against their common disabilities. The Indian can hardly stay out of it.

Many white people believe damaging and untrue things about us. For example, that the Indians are overrunning the country, or will do so. The facts are that Asiatic immigration has been prohibited since 1913, and today even a wife married overseas cannot enter the country as of right. Recently a few wives who came to join their husbands were sent back to India.

There is a lot of alarmist propaganda about the Indian birth rate. In fact there is no danger of the Indians ever exceeding the white South African population even in the year 2000. It has been estimated by a competent authority that at this date there will be 1.4 million Asiatics against 4.5 million Europeans, 3 million Coloureds, and 21 million Africans. It is not really the Indian birth rate that is the cause of this alarm, but the increasing disparity in numbers between whites and non-whites as a whole. The dilemma of the whites, which the Indian can appreciate being the tiniest minority group himself, can only be solved by unprecedented immigration. This solution is still evading the whites, and in their frustration they attack the Indian.

There is another misconception: that most Indians are merchants hoarding up enormous wealth by frugal living. This is what a recently published book by the University of Natal has to say: 'To the casual onlooker the obvious wealth of some Indian traders with well-established premises and first class fittings and stock is apt to give a wrong idea. The other side of the picture shows many small back street traders whose turnover is probably low. . . . The "locale" of many traders is in itself a serious limitation to any increase in turnover.'[1]

The author of this report (a European) also calculated that in Natal out of about 15,000 Indians engaged in commerce in 1952 only about 4,500 were owners of businesses. In the Transvaal the proportion is higher, but the Indian is mainly a petty trader. Having pioneered in the rural areas he has rendered a valuable service to the white farmer and the African peasantry. But now there has emerged a new class of retail trader amongst the Afrikaners and the Africans, and so with this additional source of commercial rivalry we can expect increased anti-Indianism.

Though there is so much hostility towards them, Indians on the whole are not inclined to leave the country and return to India. Voluntary repatriation schemes, carrying a small monetary inducement, have hitherto failed. By dint of hard work, thrift and patience they have improved upon their economic status since the days of indentured labour, in spite of heavy obstacles. In their attitude to repatriation they show the inertia of any people who have settled in a country for well nigh 100 years, and have helped to develop it. They do not see why they should be deprived of the fruits of their labour, and cast out of their homeland. Their main grievance is that

[1] *The Indian Community of Natal.* See Reading List.

they are not permitted to develop freely and to the full extent of their capacities. Newly arrived immigrants from Europe have a higher status and greater opportunities of advancement than Indians born in the country.

It is often said that Indians are better off here than they would be in India. The argument is meaningless as fourth and fifth generations Indians know nothing about conditions in India, and the only standards they know are the Western standards of South Africa. In fact the Cape Town Agreement of 1927 between India and South Africa specifically stated that Indians who desired to stay in South Africa should conform to Western standards of living.

It is becoming customary to put all the blame for Indian disabilities upon the Afrikaner Nationalists. That is not correct. Four-fifths of the Indians live in the predominantly English province of Natal. It was this province which first introduced Indians into South Africa and prospered by their labour. I do not want to belabour this point, but the following extract from the report of an all-English Natal Committee on Post-War Works and Reconstruction should give a clue to the prevailing English way of looking at us: 'The Indian of the labouring, peasant, and employee class is serving a useful purpose, but the Indian of the more affluent classes is a menace to European civilization in Natal. . . .'

With the steady improvement in their educational and economic status Indians naturally desired to live in better surroundings, and since these were the monopoly of the Europeans they bought properties in these areas. This led to raising the cry of 'Indian penetration' and culminated in the Group Areas Act. In the plans already proposed to the Group Areas Board by the City Council, huge areas of Durban predominantly settled by Indians have been allocated for the occupation and ownership of Europeans and Coloureds. The

Indians will be thrust out into the undeveloped areas on the perimeter of the city. The land offered is in the ownership of Europeans mostly, and the present market price is far in excess of what the Indians had paid for their present holdings. This Act will hit not only the Indian mercantile element but also thousands of houseowners and smallholders, whose houses and holdings represent their entire life savings. There is, of course, little publicity given to this gigantic white penetration.

Now what of Indian relations to the African? You will have read about the disastrous riot of 1949 in Durban when Africans attacked Indians, setting fire to Indian shops and houses and causing many casualties. In the racial hierarchy of privileges the Indian is just above the African, and in most things of life in the urban areas they are thrown very much together. Rising African nationalism and frustration makes its attacks upon the group next above it, encouraged very much by the anti-Indianism of the whites. But the Africans who took part actively in the riots were drawn from the elements which had the least stake in urban life. They were male migrant labourers compelled to live in celibacy in the labour compounds, or miserably housed shack dwellers on the outskirts of the city, and many unemployed, desperate people. The educated Africans who lived with their families in well-planned African housing schemes had little to do with this rioting.

In his attitude to the African, the Indian makes a clear distinction between the backward, tribally orientated African and the urbanized Western orientated and educated African.

Quite unlike the European, the Indian does not fear the educational and economic and even political advancement of the African. If power is ultimately to be transferred to the African, they would certainly like this to be transferred to persons whose mode of living and thinking is of the twentieth century, and are capable of continuing government along modern, democratic lines; and one does not see the possibility of Africans acquiring this experience unless they are inducted into the practice of government now. In short, the Indian minority believes that its own security can only be guaranteed by the advancement of the African.

I have tried to give some frank impressions about the relations of my own people to Europeans and to Africans. Now I must say something about what one could call our domestic affairs – Indian politics. The two major political groupings are the South African Indian Organisation and the South African Indian Congress. The first is a conservative group, representative largely of mercantile and propertied interests. It continues to place faith in the policy of presenting memoranda, and seeking interviews with government Ministers and officials, to secure a redress of Indian grievances. It tries to save as much as possible of Indian interests by putting forward to the Group Areas Board alternative race zoning plans and this policy compels it to bargain with the segregationists. As you may imagine, in these activities it is painfully aware of the political impotence of the Indian minority. It is also understandable that its policy is seen by some as 'collaboration'.

The other and rival body, the Indian Congress, is led by young university-trained professionals and men hardened in the trade union movement. This body has taken over and employed the passive resistance technique of the late Mahatma Gandhi, and the mass rally and demonstration techniques of the leftists. It undertakes the political education of its cadres. It does not feel politically impotent, for its analysis of the racial situation here leads it to join forces with the African political movement, and in the general anti-colonial movement led by the Afro-Asian group of nations. It is conscious of the political power latent in organized non-white labour. Its leaders courted imprisonment during the passive resistance campaigns of 1946 and 1952. Today many of them have been banned by the Government under the Suppression of Communism Act. In December 1956 several of these were arrested and at the time of going to press are undergoing a preparatory examination on a charge of high treason. Communism is defined somewhat widely in South African law. The Congress members are non-violently aggressive against the racial laws, but they are definitely not anti-white, because so many of them have a stake in the continuation of the Western way of life here. The whole purpose of their agitation is to achieve equality with the dominant white group, and to participate in the decisions that govern their lives and properties. There are some communists amongst their supporters, attracted to communism as a reaction to the colour bar.

Things look very dark just now for the Indian. By temperament and training he does not like violence. He has been trying to persuade the African to keep to the path of non-violence, and the 1952 Defiance Campaign called by the African National Congress was conducted along non-violent lines. But one cannot be sure whether the African, who carries a heavier burden than the Indian, would be able to contain himself.

I do not think the present policy of *apartheid* will succeed because it is much too late, too costly, and its hypothetical benefits to the African too remote. Because it really perpetuates white supremacy *apartheid* is a provocative challenge to all Asia and Africa. We can appreciate the fears and anxieties of the white minority. But a gradual approach to sharing life in a common society is the only wise alternative. The Indian minority, after all, has come much closer than the European ever will to the nightmare of engulfment by another and different race, and we know that the end may not be so terrible after all when the standards of living and the cultural values of the different racial groups converge – and there is much convergence already. Being so much closer to the African, we also know that something must be done soon to remove the fears and prejudices which strangulate African advancement, and which thereby endanger the lives of us all.

19

THE COLOURED PEOPLE

by R. E. van der Ross

am a Cape Coloured person in South Africa. That is, I am not
nything which is not Coloured. I am not European, or
Native, or Indian or Chinese. This makes the position rather
omplicated, and the definition somewhat circular. You will
notice that I find it easier to say what I am not than to say what
am. In this I follow our legislators, who have found them-
elves in this quandary whenever they have tried to define the
Coloured people. However, one must eliminate the hair-
plitting and make the assumption that the Coloured people, as
group, do exist. This assumption confers status on the
Coloured people and existence on myself, and so, having at
nce a subject and a speaker, we are able to proceed.

When Jan van Riebeeck arrived at the Cape in 1652 to
stablish a provision station in order to promote trade with the
East, he brought about 100 men and very few women from
Holland. The result was that mixture and marriage between the
Dutch and visiting sailors and the aboriginal people, and later
mported slaves, was encouraged. The result of all this mixing
as been the Coloured people. That the process of 'racial
nixing' as it is called has not died out yet is proved by the
eed found by the Government to enact not only the Mixed
Marriages Act, but also the Immorality Act, which makes
legal certain forms of immorality only if practised between
white and non-white. That these have not been effective, and

are not likely to be, is proved by a recent statement by a magistrate of Stellenbosch, centre of Nationalist culture, that for a town of its size the incidence of convictions under the Immorality Act is alarmingly high! In any case, the inference that immorality is condoned if restricted to members of the same racial group is a dangerous one for any society.

I am not going to enter into a description of all phases of the life of my people. This would largely be unnecessary, for, in spite of the appellation 'Coloured', we are still people and carry on all the normal activities of a modern society. Of the $1\frac{1}{4}$ million, some 80% live in the Western Cape and about 65% in the towns. The fact that a generation ago only 46% lived in the towns shows how rapid the process of urbanization is.

When I say that we carry on all the activities of a normal society, I should qualify this by adding 'as far as we are permitted'. For, although we till the soil, milk the cows, tend the sheep, cultivate the vine and fruit trees, sow the corn and reap the harvest; although in the towns we make roads, drive trucks, construct buildings, mind machines, hawk vegetables and trade in a small way, teach the young, nurse the sick and so on, there are things which we are not allowed to do, either by law or by circumstances arising out of the law.

For example, you will not find Coloured persons in senior positions in government departments, or in legislative positions. You will not find them employed as university professors or as hospital superintendents, or as engine drivers or as top-grade technicians on government contracts. In private concerns you will rarely find them employed in positions such as salesmen where they may come into contact with white customers. The critic will say that these positions will be opened up as the Coloured people accept *apartheid* and develop in their own areas. But I am at the moment describing things as they are. In some of the cases cited above the reason for exclusion is that th aw prohibits it. In other cases there is custom and practice. Custom and practice are, however, largely themselves the result of growing up in an atmosphere determined by law. At least, this is so in South Africa, where I feel that the normal procedure of having the customs and desires of the people determine the law is reversed, and we find the people (that is, the minority, some three million white people) having their destiny shaped for them along lines of colour prejudice, and being convinced by a fear, induced by emotion and supported by arithmetic, that unless they accept the pattern of thinking of white superiority they are doomed to extinction. Having accepted this assumption they leave the business of governing to the Government and hope for the best.

It is commonly said that the Coloured people are a divided people. I am not qualified to say whether this division is a real and essential cause of political or economic disability. I do not agree that unity or oneness necessarily promotes progress any more than I agree that my mobility would be increased by having one leg, rather than the customary two. What is far more important is that the groups or sub-groups should have sufficient unity of purpose to be able to move in a generally agreed direction.

But what are these divisions? Division or grouping is no peculiarly Cape Coloured or even South African phenomenon. The Coloured people have sub-groups of varying degrees of coherence and exclusiveness. In a country in which colour weighs so heavily, it is not surprising that colour is a major criterion for these divisions within the Coloured group itself. Two other criteria are money and educational status.

Having learnt as much as we have from the white South Africans we have not been slow to acquire their vices too. One of the chief of these is colour prejudice. In physical appearance the Coloured people range from those indistinguishable from

Africans on one hand, to those indistinguishable from Europeans on the other. Being white in South Africa qualifies one for numerous privileges, and it is therefore understandable that to some people, who have the necessary physical qualifications in regard to pigmentation, features, hair form and texture, etc., being white represents the epitome of achievement. And once one has gained acceptance (however precarious) into the ranks of the whites, one regards it as one's first duty to safeguard this achievement for oneself and one's children.

Very often this process of safeguarding one's position entails severing connections with previous associates to whom one is known as Coloured. This means that one has to break off old friendships, leave the district where one has grown up, and in many cases it has even meant leaving the country. I do not wish to go into the question of personal and inward suffering which this state must entail. The breaking of old associations is at no time easy, and then there is the constant dread of discovery. Every Coloured person, in the towns particularly, could tell of numerous cases of people who have 'turned white' – and who have not gained the sympathy of their erstwhile friends in doing so. The many cases on record of divisions within families, often with tragic, always with unhappy results, represent but a small part of the many actual such cases.

One must, however, be fair, and I do not suggest that every case of play-whiteism is motivated by race prejudice or by a lack of loyalty, whatever that may mean. It is possible that some of these people take the point of view that they, as individuals, do not intend to go through life bearing the stigma of Colour. They may contend that they wish to live as free men and women, and that, in South Africa, the nearest approach to this is to be white. And if one cannot be free in South Africa, one goes overseas in search of freedom. And let there be no doubt that when I speak of the stigma of Colour I mean just that. Society has so deeply shown its disfavour of the Coloured person by differential treatment, that to be Coloured is not regarded as an honour except by the dogged few. Some time ago, when a man prosecuted under the Immorality Act pleaded that he was, in fact, Coloured and not European, the magistrate said 'If he chooses to be Coloured, let him be branded as Coloured forever.' And I noticed recently that someone had been granted £150 damages by another magistrate because he was called Coloured.

He might well be awarded damages, because he could suffer very real loss by being called Coloured. And this is loss not only to social prestige, but in other ways, too. He could be debarred from purchasing or occupying certain property under the Group Areas Act. He could be debarred from marrying whom he wanted under the Mixed Marriages Act. His employers might consider it harmful to have a Coloured person in their employ and so he might lose his work. His children could be debarred from attending certain schools, technical colleges or universities. Should he wish to travel in South Africa he would be severely handicapped in regard to travel facilities on the railways, accommodation at hotels, and so on. In the course of his daily travel to and from work by public transport he would have to suffer the indignity of travelling in specially labelled coaches, and often the humiliation of less courteous treatment and the inconvenience of less comfortable facilities.

It is true that some of these restrictions cut both ways, that is that Europeans are also debarred from certain places reserved for non-Europeans. But it is also true that, almost without exception, the advantages in respect of number and quality of facility are all on the side of the Europeans.

The most urgent and difficult problem facing the thinking

Coloured person today is: What to do and how to advise others in the face of increasing *apartheid*. Leaving emotional politics and political emotionalism aside, there is the sober fact to face that the policy of *apartheid* is being practised more and more widely by the day. Should the *bona fides* of the Government be accepted? Is the record of the past such that we may accept it? Should the people build up opposition? Are the necessary conditions for effective opposition there? Dare we tell the young people, particularly, not to avail themselves of separate facilities and so possibly be party to their being only frustrated, poorly qualified and, therefore, more easily exploited?

On the other hand, dare we recommend an acceptance of the *apartheid* principle and co-operate in its implementation on the very meagre evidence of good faith thus far given? Supposing time should reveal that this trust of ours has been misplaced. And there is the further question, whether our co-operation is desired at all. I mean, real co-operation, where each party assists the other and takes the good advice of the other, not co-operation which means that one party accepts whilst the other dictates; the co-operation of co-workers and companions and not of puppets.

These are the questions uppermost in our minds, and the difficulty in answering them consistently in word and in deed has led many to despair and to desert the political field. The difficulty is increased by knowing that the responsibility is great, for unborn generations will have to live in the world now being created.

In regard to political, as distinct from social, division amongst the Coloured people, these are not as many as some would pretend. It is true that there have been many political organizations, but if one looks for real divisions of conviction so deep as to hold no hope of eventual co-operation, one would look in vain.

What we are suffering from at the moment is more of a clash of personalities and the result of unfortunate over-statement and unbridled emotionalism of the past ten or fifteen years. During those years we had the political leadership mainly in the hands of teachers. As a member of that esteemed profession, I am only too aware of, first, its luxuriant verbosity and, second, of its vulnerability to pressure from governmental quarters. As a result of the pressure, the political group fell back on the verbosity. In other words, it felt strongly about the political situation, as is only to be expected, since it is the only considerable group of any intellectual achievement within the Coloured people. But by this same token, being teachers, they were unable to take action commensurately strong. Hence they resorted to strong talking. And, because they were trying to gain a following from the rank and file, they were compelled to choose as targets for their invective persons close to the rank and file. The result was an outbreak of personal abuse and boycott of other Coloured leaders.

This has led to some very bitter feelings. But they are at most feelings restricted to certain small groups, and it is difficult to keep them alive, even if anyone wanted to. The last few years have seen a very decided decrease in their hold. We have seen more people coming into political leadership from the ranks of non-teachers in clerks, factory workers, trade unionists. There is a growing realization that, in the eyes of the law, all Coloured people are Coloured, and we will gain nothing by accentuating differences ourselves. In other words, whilst different sub-groups remain, all are coming to greater agreement on the general direction in which we should steer.

There is also a growing realization that the destiny of the Coloured person is linked with that of the African. People who ten years ago would have recoiled in horror from the thought of associating with the African in any way, now accept it as axiomatic that we have to seek bonds of friendship with him. That this is so is no doubt due to the fact that the white man appears to show in no uncertain way that he does not desire our co-operation and friendship. Whether this is true or not, the fact is that this is how the Coloured people interpret the recent flood of *apartheid* legislation.

There is a final question relevant to this matter of division and which is asked by many inside and outside South Africa today. It is this: Why were the Coloured people so silent at a time when their rights were being threatened and, indeed, removed?

There are two answers to the question. The first is that they were in reality not quiet. The public memory is short. The past few years, since the matter of our vote was raised in 1950, have been years of strenuous political activity. There have been meetings, demonstrations, deputations and all other impedimenta of political campaigning on a large scale. Political groups which had never met before met on common platforms, and at least one new political organization was born.

But if the question is asked why this activity was not evident in the most recent chapter of the crisis, when the Coloured voter was actually removed from the common roll, the answer must flow out of what I have just said.

We did all these things. We appealed to history, to tradition, to the law, to past promises and to keeping faith. We failed. We realized that we are dealing with persons not prepared to depart one step from a predetermined course. We did not depart from our principles and convictions. We did not lack courage or energy. Posterity needs to know that we of this generation did not give up without a fight. That fight we have fought and lost. We lost it because the opposition had better legal weapons than we had, and was prepared to create others f needs be. We did not see the faintest possibility of success at his stage.

This does not mean that we must reject our principles. But it does, in my opinion, mean that we shall have to turn the new position to our best advantage, that we shall have to use the benefits and weaknesses of *apartheid* in all its aspects so that we become stronger than before. It means a conscientious application to improvement in educational attainment and entrenchment in industry. In this growing country, that is where our ultimate strength lies. Already we are an indispensable factor in the industry of the Cape. We must become the governing factor there. Towards this end all our forces must be inspanned. If *apartheid* is a myth and incapable of achievement, we must prove it to be so. And I believe that the best way to prove this is to take our full place, even if our presence is somewhat unwelcome, in the process of developing the country of our birth. For that is the status to which we aspire, the status of being, not just 'the Coloured people', but full South Africans.

READING LIST

An African Survey by the Rt. Hon. the Lord Hailey, G.C.S.I., G.C.M.G. G.C.I.E. Oxford University Press for Royal Institute of International Affairs, 1957.

Perspectives in Human Malnutrition by T. and J. Gillman. Grune and Stratton, New York, 1951.

Vitamins in Theory and Practice by L. J. Harris. Cambridge University Press, 1955.

Patterns of Health and Nutrition in South African Bantu by S. L. Kark. Witwatersrand University Press, 1954.

African Intelligence by S. Biesheuvel. South African Institute of Race Relations, 1945.

Some Economic Problems of the Bantu in South Africa by D. H. Houghton. South African Institute of Race Relations, 1939.

The Economy of a Native Reserve (Keiskammahoek Rural Survey Vol. II) by D. H. Houghton and E. M. Walton. Shuter and Shooter, Pietermaritzburg, 1952.

Native Labour in South Africa by N. N. Franklin. Oxford University Press, 1954.

The African Factory Worker: a sample study of the life and labour of the urban African worker by S. B. Nycobo, B. Nomvete and others. Oxford University Press for the University of Natal, 1950.

Report of the Commission on Industrial Legislation 1951, Union Government 62–51. Public Printer, Pretoria.

African Urbanisation in Ndola and Luanshya by J. C. Mitchell. Rhodes Livingstone Communication No. 6, 1954.

Marriage, Bridewealth and Women in an African Society by J. F. Holleman. Rhodes-Livingstone Paper No. 26, 1956.

The Administration of Justice and the Urban African by A. L. Epstein. Colonial Research Series No. 7, H.M.S.O., 1953.

The Indian Community of Natal (Natal Regional Survey, Vol. IX) by C. A. Woods. Oxford University Press, 1954.

Colour and Culture in South Africa by S. Patterson. Routledge and Kegan Paul, 1953.

Integration or Separate Development. South African Bureau of Racial Affairs, Stellenbosch, 1952.

Apartheid – A Slogan or a Solution. South African Bureau of Racial Affairs, Stellenbosch, 1954.

Handbook on Race Relations in South Africa by E. Hellman. Oxford University Press, 1949.

Racial Laws versus Economic and Social Forces by E. Hellman. South African Institute of Race Relations, 1955.

Date Due

MAR 12 '65		
APR 22 '65		
MAR 22 '69		
APR 3 '69		
FEB 22 '72		
APR 28 '85		
APR 6		
	PRINTED IN U. S. A.	